Mind Your P's & Qs

Mind Your Ps & Qs

✦

How to achieve Quality through Process Improvement: a handbook for humans.

David Covey

iUniverse, Inc.
New York Lincoln Shanghai

Mind Your Ps & Qs
How to achieve Quality through Process Improvement: a handbook for humans.

iUniverse, Inc.

For information address:
iUniverse, Inc.
2021 Pine Lake Road, Suite 100
Lincoln, NE 68512
www.iuniverse.com

ISBN: 0-595-27754-3

Printed in the United States of America

This book is dedicated to all those people who have unwittingly provided me with both the material and the motive to write it.

Human history becomes more and more a race between education and
catastrophe.

—H. G. Wells

Contents

Preface

A couple of years ago, I was working in an office building that was being fitted out and where—apart from the reception area on each floor—there was nowhere to hang coats. So, I would take mine to my office and lay it on a chair, or somewhere it was easily to hand. The building is fitted with those sun-sensitive blinds which automatically go up and down, but unfortunately those outside my own office had been taken down for repair due to storm damage.

One winter day, it still being dark when I arrived, I switched on the halogen floor-standing lamp and got on with my work. Mid-morning, the sun started to shine in, bringing with it a problem for me of reflections in my monitor screen. I maneuvered the floor lamp around so that it was between me and the sun, carefully arranged my raincoat over the wide, upward-facing lamp shade and—congratulating myself on being just about as clever as you could get—went back to my work.

A while later, I noticed a strange smell. I wasn't sure what it was, but as my office was (strategically I believe) across the corridor from the Men's Room, I screwed up my nose and carried on with my work. Some time after that, a colleague came in and asked if I could smell burning. I replied that, yes, I could smell *something* but that I had no idea what it was. Luckily for me, he wasn't about to lose the scent and sniffed around, hound-like. Nostrils twitching wildly, he literally followed his nose to my raincoat, which was smoldering nicely across the lamp…

Not for the first time—and surely not for the last—I provided living proof of my thesis that ours is the most stupid species on the planet. This is in spite of our being able—unlike others—to quickly recognize, and correct, our mistakes. Other species take a lot longer to do this, for some the route to enlightenment can take centuries. (*Well, I did tell him to watch out for those big hairy things with the enormous teeth…*)

Despite this ability to learn quickly, we still tend to *not* learn from our mistakes but rather to compound them. It is this inherent capacity for stupidity, and its effects on quality in particular, which I am seeking to address.

♦   ♦   ♦

There are many books dealing with one or other aspect of "quality". There are many standards, theories, models; and you will find articles on the subject in virtually any trade magazine you pick up. You can attend seminars on *Total Quality Management* anywhere and everywhere. We spend so much time talking about it that we are surely all now experts in quality…Yet how often do we practice that which is preached at us daily?

I don't intend to preach, rather to write the kind of book I would have found helpful when I started out trying to improve the quality of R&D processes. Everything you read here is based on my own observations and experience in various programs and projects in several companies, large and not so large. That experience has been mostly, but not exclusively, in system and software development, but I believe that the principles described here might be advantageously applied to improving just about any process-rich endeavor.

Although recent experience elsewhere has reinforced my belief that it can equally well apply to other areas, *Mind Your Ps & Qs* was originally intended for anyone managing, involved in, or affected by what we might loosely call "hi-tech" development. It particularly addresses the problems that make efforts to improve quality in R&D both costly and unpopular. I have seen these "evergreen" problems time and time again over the years in different companies, and the chances are that they are affecting your own organization's efforts to improve right now.

♦   ♦   ♦

I say to people that I get paid for stating the obvious(usually not right away to the people paying me). I hope that having read this book, it will all be obvious to you too, as I share with you some secrets that you probably already know. I will try to bring things together—*quality, improvements, business needs, customer and market pressures, intra-organization communications and more*—in a way which offers an inclusive and pragmatic perspective.

Sometimes, it's simply that you are so engaged in the day-to-day fight to stay in the race that you don't see the obvious. My aim is to help you take an objective look at your own organization and help you to assure your customers get what they want not just this time, but *every time*.

David Covey

My thanks go to Don Anderson, Lynn Annan, Horst Degen-Hientz, Peter Niggemeier, Sebastián Tyrrell and Michael Woods whose helpful comments and suggested improvements to my writing process are—*I hope*—reflected in the quality of the end product!

Introduction—Stating The Obvious

There are no "silver bullets" when it comes to Process Improvement. There is only hard work. Yes, there are improvement models that show you the way, but they only tell you what you've got to achieve, not how to do it. That's for you to decide.

If your roof leaks, *you* have to decide what to do about it. You might patch it. You might use something to catch the drips. You might renew the whole roof or encase your entire property in an enormous protective bubble. You could do lots of things, and some of them will be simple but effective, others costly and ineffective, in any case, it's *your* call.

Improvement models show you where it is you're headed, give you a map, and (sometimes) tell you how to read it. What I'm doing is giving you a compass and explaining how you can use it with—*or without*—your map to reach your goal. It's up to you which route you take. That's because it's *your* journey, neither I nor the authors of your chosen model will be there with you.

Having already illustrated my own qualification in the Preface, I would ask you to consider for a moment the possibility that you too might not be perfect. Not only have you done dumb things in the past, you will probably continue to do so throughout your remaining years. (If you can't believe that, then maybe this isn't the book for you—maybe you're already just too far advanced in this area. Put the book back on the shelf and try the section marked "Books for Superior Beings" instead.)

Now, I didn't do the raincoat thing I told you about *intentionally*. Nobody makes mistakes *intentionally*—mistakes are, by definition, *un*intentional. Being human, we often blame other people for their mistakes but excuse ourselves our own. I spend a lot of my time investigating problems and trying to find ways of solving, or preventing, them. People never tell me about the problems they cause for other people, only those which adversely affect them and which they see as having been caused by others.

1

The awful, inescapable, truth is that we *all* screw up. Every day of our lives. Mostly little things. Often things which, for the most part, we instantly forget because they have no significance. Until, that is, they sometimes come back to haunt us when little mistakes turn into BIG problems. How many times have you found yourself saying something like "imagine what might have happened if..." as a result of some innocuous domestic error you managed to correct in time? The door that wasn't properly shut, the window left open, the appliance left on...

When we leave home and transfer into that often pressurized environment called "work", we forget the fact that we are still human and that, *ipso facto*, errors will occur. And so, our "stupidity chips" kick into overdrive just about the same time that we walk into the office, plant, shop, wherever.

Being human, we make mistakes. Machines make mistakes because they have been made, or programmed, by humans. Machines made by machines make mistakes because humans made the machines that made them. We are now so familiar with machines that there seems to be a general perception that they have some sort of life of their own. They don't. We made them what they are. To err is human. Period...

If you have any doubts about whether your organization needs to improve how it delivers quality, my argument is very simple. Unless your organization has always totally excluded humans, then you need to constantly consider how you can eradicate the mistakes that walk in with those humans. The way you do that is by improving the way you do things. *By improving your processes.*

You have to improve your processes to the point where mistakes are so alien to your culture that when they occur they will invariably be discovered *before* they do any damage. For most organizations, it will be a long journey. Process Improvement is all about avoiding making mistakes.

Prevention rather than cure.

As you will read here, one of the first things you have to do in order to successfully implement Process Improvement, is to ensure that everyone knows what it is they are dealing with. In order to understand what I'm writing about, you first have to be aware of some definitions. I don't ask that you necessarily agree 100% with my definitions, but you should at least understand the basic premise for the book.

These are *my* answers to the questions that you must clarify for your own improvement program before you start. Your own people have to understand how the answers to these questions relate to them and to their part in your program. These aren't "frequently asked questions", rather the "rarely get asked questions" which people *don't* ask because they don't want to appear stupid.

- *What is Quality?*
- *What is Process?*
- *What is the relationship between Quality and Process?*
- *What is Process Improvement?*
- *What is Quality Improvement?*

What is "Quality"?

There are many definitions of "quality" and when talking to people about the subject, I usually start by looking at the things it is *not*, because we do use the word in quite different ways. For example, it is often used to indicate luxury or opulence, and those other uses of the word do tend to confuse people.

There are also different definitions of the word when used in the business context of producing things, but the one I prefer is this…

"Quality is conformance to requirements."

I like this definition because it's simple and relatively easy to understand once you accept that quality is discrete and measurable. It also maintains the link with the reason we are seeking to build quality into our products, namely, in order to meet our customer's requirements, i.e. to give them what they want.

Different customers will have different requirements and expectations, but remember that there aren't different levels of quality, just different levels of service or functionality. "Quality" is *always* whatever is required. So, while your customers might accept different levels of *features* in a product or service, if it doesn't meet their expectations of that level of service then they will complain. Or just not come back…

You need to think of Quality in a very wide sense and recognize that it embraces everything that you do in developing your product to ensure that it meets the requirements. Including—but not as some think *exclusively*—making sure the thing works before you ship it.

Quality is never having to say you're sorry…

What is "Process"?

"Process", put simply, means "the way you do things".

For example, if you're making a door then there are a number of steps you will take that will affect whether the door conforms to requirements. An effective process will produce a "quality" door which conforms to requirements rather than a "non-quality" door which falls off the first time it's opened, doesn't fit, and so on.

What you do at work *is* process. If you produce things, then you will—even if they might not be so defined—use processes. Processes for design, manufacture, materials handling, tooling, and so on. In order to assure quality, you have to monitor your processes against something—guidelines, templates, measurements, etc.

When considering processes, you also need to consider what else impacts on the way you do things—tools, systems, service contracts, working environments—as these may need to be improved too. Sometimes, these ancillary things can have a massively negative or positive effect on your core processes.

What is the relationship between Quality and Process?

Think of Quality as what you want to achieve and Process as the way you will achieve it. "I want to give my customer what (s)he wants and this is how I'll do it." It's almost that simple, but in practice there has to be the additional element of constancy. You have to have a *defined* way of achieving quality; otherwise you won't be able to repeat your successes. (Or avoid repeating your mistakes.)

So, Quality is what you want to get and your processes should be a *defined and constant* way of achieving it.

Before we can talk about improvement, we must distinguish between product and process. Product is what you get from applying your processes. It follows that with this split we can talk about two types of quality—product[1] quality and process quality.

Product Quality is how we ensure that the product conforms to requirements—and that's done largely through the application of processes. A "requirement" for product quality would typically be a set of parameters, measures, and so on, perhaps embodied in a product specification. In other words, what the customer expects to get.

Process Quality is how we make sure that our processes are working in a defined and constant way that will support Product Quality. Usually, comparing the effectiveness of our processes against an improvement model or standard will

---

1.   Or "service" if that's what you're doing.

do this. (This is because the quality of processes themselves depends on their being useable and robust enough to be consistently and constantly applied.)

What is "Process Improvement"?

Process Improvement means ensuring that the way you do things is defined, practiced and optimized so that the product you're developing by using those processes will conform to requirements.

You might expect that it stands to reason that if you improve your processes then you should improve your quality, but not necessarily. It's not so unusual for apparent improvements in one area of the process to have a negative effect elsewhere. Such is life, and that's why Process Improvement is best done as a combined effort across all areas in the organization where processes affect Product Quality.

You also need to ensure that your improvements actually are *improvements* and not just change for change's sake. That means you have to have a basis for making each improvement and a definite, measurable, goal for that improvement. (You'll find more about this later, suffice to say that you must know *why* you're making improvements and how you'll measure whether they've been a success.)

This book seeks to explain how to set about improving your applied processes in order to minimize the likelihood of errors impacting the quality of the product you deliver.

What is "Quality Improvement"?

Quality Improvement is when you improve the way you ensure that your customer gets what they want. That means motivating your workforce to understand, analyze and correct anything which has an adverse effect on quality, including—*but not confined to*—processes. Although what you do is process, and therefore can be defined as such, there are other things which affect quality that cannot be simply defined in terms of process. For example, workplace layout affects staff morale and, therefore, quality.

Although for development areas it might be argued that Quality Improvement and Process Improvement are the same, it is important to at least recognize that there is a difference in the way they may be perceived. If you are in R & D and work closely with a manufacturing function, you will need to consider how your process improvements affect the overall Product Quality, and how they fit with any ongoing improvement program which may well not be process-oriented.

◆   ◆   ◆

One more thing. It's important to recognize from the outset that nobody is to blame if your organization needs to improve. You have to improve and that's all there is to it. How you got to that state doesn't matter a jot compared to what you intend to do about it. You might have your suspicions about particular individuals' contribution to your mess, but look on the bright side—you can make sure it doesn't happen again.

If your idea of improving things is to find out who's to blame then things won't improve. You're all in this together...

◆   ◆   ◆

So, although you might not like to admit it, you are *not* perfect, you're *human*. You make mistakes, you make assumptions, and you make problems for others. To put not too fine a point on it, you too can screw up. And, if you screw up, the chances are the way you do things is screwed up too...

Truths And Home Truths

I am rather assuming that if you're reading a book about improving quality, then you've already identified a need to do so in your own organization or are simply interested in knowing more about how to do it.

If you're *not* yet convinced about whether you need to start an improvement program in your own organization, it's easy enough to find out whether you do. Probably, the very fact that you *think* you might need to is enough. You need to improve if your processes aren't producing what is required when it is required. If that is the case, then there is room for improvement and benefits to be had—cost savings, faster time to market, lower staff turnover, less sleepless nights…

You may already see lots of reasons to improve or none at all. Often, people get so used to avoiding problems by ignoring them or working around them, that eventually they forget there ever was a problem. That doesn't mean it has gone away though, and it will be costing you more to *not* address the problem than it would to face up to it and find a lasting solution. Your perception of problems in process areas is also colored by your own expectations and experience. If you've become used to workarounds and high error rates, then that's probably what you would consider "normal".

I don't believe there is any such thing as "normal". There are no normal people, no normal weather, and no normal behavior. There are *norms*, but if you're saying things like "well, that's normal for us" you're really saying "we admitted defeat on this a long time ago". If you expect to be "normal", then that's what you'll be and your results will reflect your way of thinking. If you can accept the fact that something can *always* be done better, quicker, faster, cheaper, *whateverer,* then you're on your way to improving.

Having said there's no such thing as normal, there are still plenty of ways you can measure your process efficiency. There are subjective methods (of which the "is this to our usual standard?" approach is one) and more objective ones—international standards, process maturity models etc. Bear in mind that even these may not be truly objective, as they rely on human judgment. An auditor or assessor makes interpretations based on his or her experience, and everyone's experience is different.

If you're not yet convinced of the need to improve, you will be able to find something suitable that will allow you to objectively measure the effectiveness of your endeavors. Although it's best to spend some time to get to know improvement models, in a lot of cases a few hours is enough to allow you insight into how your processes measure up, and whether the model is likely to be right for your purposes.

As long as you can't honestly say that you're producing fault-free products from error-free processes, then there's room for improvement.

If you're an adherent of the "yes, but this is the *real* world Dave" school of restrictive thought, then I can offer some *real world* experience for you to consider.

Your agreeing to any of the following is symptomatic of process disease. This being the *real world* and all, I'll have to ask you to trust me when I say in my *real world* experience that if you do answer "YES", then you need to consider the possibility that you have a need for Process Improvement. There are plenty of other questions I could ask, but these usually do the trick.

- *Do you see testing as the way you make sure the product is as fault-free as possible?*

Testing should prove that the product does what is expected. If your view of testing is that it is primarily a way to find bugs, then you should consider the fact that somewhere prior to testing your processes are letting those bugs in. Concentrate on stopping them at source by improving your processes.

- *Because of the nature of our projects, it's impossible to plan in any detail. We believe in dynamic management!*

If you can't plan ahead then either you're too lazy to, don't know how to or—quite likely—your processes don't give you a basis for trustworthy plans, i.e. you probably have only a vague idea in advance what will be produced and when. (But this is all new stuff, so nobody can plan that can they? Yeah, right…)

- *Do you have to "chase" people for information or work results? Are others constantly pestering you for information that you simply don't know yet?*

Good processes enable good communications. Poor processes mean you can never quite trust what you're told. So everybody wastes a lot of time in meetings, discussions and "workshops". (There are workshops and there are "workshops".

If your workshops tend to be unscheduled problem—solving sessions then consider holding a workshop on how to avoid problems!)

• *Do you think your boss just doesn't understand what it is that you do and that if only (s)he did, then you wouldn't have to spend so much of your time explaining?*

Well-defined and mature processes mean that people can rely on what will be produced by those processes. If management have the devil's own job getting information from the process (e.g. from reliable plans) then they will have to turn to you because you probably ARE the process.

• *If only everybody else did his or her job as well as I do mine, we wouldn't have any problem.*

Yup, it's those others all right. Especially the finicky ones who find all those stupid little bugs and things. Hey! Nobody's perfect, right?

• *Some of our work simply can't be described by way of processes.*

One of those things wouldn't be "Design" by any chance would it? Or gathering customer requirements?

Some processes are inherently creative, and describing them—let alone defining them—is difficult. But not impossible. Though it won't be easy, you have to have an agreed framework for such activities. It mustn't be constraining and can start as something very simple, but there have to be "rules" for such creative areas, otherwise the input to other processes (and therefore quality) will be fundamentally flawed. If you don't describe all your process areas, you're simply evading the issue, and it's just those "difficult" areas which are probably the ones causing you the most problems…

• *Even if we're not perfect, we always get there in the end.*

Maybe, but probably not exactly where you intended to get to. *And at what cost?*

Ps And Qs?

Every management guidebook has to have a snappy acronym or easy to understand method which might stand a chance of circumventing our stupidity chips, at least until the next book we read. As if you haven't got enough to remember from all those other books! I like to think that this one's easy, as I didn't have to go through any complex linguistic shenanigans to make it fit. The idea just came to me in the bath one day[1] and soon became part of the family.

"Mind your Ps & Qs"—what could be easier to remember than that? It was a rhetorical question...

Perhaps you can remember how, as a child, you were warned before you went out in public in your Sunday Best to "mind your Ps & Qs"? You probably never had any idea what the proverbial "Ps" and "Qs" were, but the warning tended to be enough. Even if it might not work quite as well today, I hope you can understand that this was a warning—you were being told to be on your very best behavior.

I'm going to ask you to do the same in order to ensure that not you, but your organization, will be on its best behavior. Throughout the book, I will describe specific Ps and Qs, which are intended to help you in your quest to reach the Holy Grail of giving your customers what they want. Failing that, at least what you think they want...

Roles

One of the things which motivated me to complete this book, was the fact that I see a real need to make sure that *everyone* plays their part in Process Improvement. I have seen initiatives falter, or fail, because of one or other of the main players not playing their part. To succeed, Process Improvement programs have

---

1. Why do ideas always appear in baths or showers? Is there any research available about this phenomenon? Maybe R&D departments should be housed in giant bathtubs. You only have to see how few really good ideas people had before baths were invented to see how true this is.

to have the active involvement, albeit sometimes in a support role, of everyone in the organization. Too often, people step back from, don't accept, or just don't know that they have, responsibilities in Process Improvement programs.

I have used the following—fairly loose and debatable—terms to encompass the roles which have to be filled in any Process Improvement program:

- **Policymakers**—the people who hold sway over whether your program will work because they have the power to say "YAY" or "NAY".

- **Managers**—the folks in the middle who have to do all that tedious stuff like meet other peoples' budgets, meet other peoples' deadlines, not have heart failure every time somebody else's problem is dumped in their lap…

- **Practitioners**—the techies or operators and the people who support them. (I started off using the term "developers" but that is somewhat restrictive. Whatever you call them, these are your "process users".)

- **Improvers**—the people who will facilitate the program, usually a dedicated team assigned for part (preferably all) of their time to support work on Process Improvement issues, specifically in implementation of changes. (I know it's not a particularly inspired choice of name, but it was the best I could come up with. Feel free to call them what you will.)

These roles apply regardless of the size of your program.

That means **regardless of size**. Sure as eggs is eggs, there will be people reading this who will say, "well, of course, we don't have to worry about [insert role or roles here]". You *do*. Unless you're doing this entirely alone in a one-person company, you have to fill all those roles. Maybe you will have to do some thinking about who they actually are in your organization, but they are there, and they have to be identified.

You will find more about each role later on.

Four Peas and a Queue

For any Process Improvement program to succeed, as well as all of those with a part to play (Policymakers, Managers, Practitioners, Improvers) doing their bit, there has to be some commonly understood form to the program itself. There are some Ps and Qs that apply to the program as a whole and without which success will be difficult to achieve.

These are:

- PREPARE
- QUANTIFY
- PREACH QUALITY
- PERSEVERE
- PEOPLE

Although some of these *can* be logically ordered, there is no specific ordering to this list, it simply reflects the order of the corresponding narrative chapters which follow. You should therefore consider these elements not as separate entities in a chain, but rather as parts of one of those very simple jigsaw puzzles for small children. Each piece has some recognizable meaning in itself, but it's only when you put them together that you see the whole picture.

Pertinent Questions (PQs)

These are questions, which you need to be asking—and working out the answers to—in order to progress. Rather than just telling you to "do this, do that", I want you to work out for yourself what needs to be done. If you can resolve a question to your *own* satisfaction in the context of your organization and what it does, then *you* will have a basis for moving forward.

Although I find the same problems in different organizations, the approaches to solving those differs—sometimes greatly.

Find honest answers to the PQs and implement your solutions in a constant, controlled way and review their success. That way you will not only improve your processes but also learn how to improve your improvement processes!

Responsibility Tables

One aim I had for *Mind Your Ps & Qs* was to avoid it looking like an instruction manual with lots of tables, figures, sub-headings and so on. I hope I've achieved that and so you will be able to read this like you would a "normal" book. Something you can read on the plane without immediately identifying yourself as the kind of sad b******* who takes their work on holiday with them. I've had to reach a compromise with myself, however, and the PQs are brought together at the end of each chapter in what I've called a "Responsibility Table". Each

Responsibility Table is meant to make you think about your own responsibilities with regard to the chapter's contents.

The Responsibility Table gives each PQ a weighting against the four roles I've identified—Policymakers, Managers, Practitioners and Improvers. What the weightings do is to assign responsibility for making sure the PQ is addressed to one or more of the roles. Mostly, they are split across two or more roles, ensuring that everyone who needs to is at least involved in addressing the PQ, but in nearly every case there is a clear-cut overall responsibility on one role.

The weightings I have awarded to each PQ requirement are based on my own experience and you may change them as you see fit. I believe my numbers can serve as the basis for initial completion of the table by any organization, certainly any *development* organization. (If you're reading this and contemplating improvements, then you probably need all the help you can get, at least to start off with.)

Appendix A—Responsibility Table brings all of these together in one composite table which may be used as an aid to identifying responsibilities within your own organization. It also describes how to use the table as preparation for your planning. All that should come later—read the book first and use each chapter's Responsibility Table as food for thought as you develop your ideas on how to implement your own improvement program.

An example Responsibility Table can be found on the next page.

Example Responsibility Table

Requirement ↓	Role → Policymakers	Managers	Practitioners	Improvers
I've used the term "Requirement" because that's what it is—a *requirement* to make sure the Pertinent Questions (PQs) you will find in each chapter are satisfactorily answered. You will have to identify how the requirement relates to your organization. Here's an example—	[Note 1] 10 points are split between each of the improvement roles defined in this book.			
PQ09—How will we fit our program to the organization with maximum benefit and minimum upset?	4	2	1	3

Note to Table

[Note 1]—I used 10 as the basis for weighting to keep life simple. Although the importance of each requirement will differ between organizations, they are all of *equal* importance to the success of your improvement program. Only whole numbers are used.

Prepare

There is a military saying—"time spent in reconnaissance is seldom wasted". One of the keys to successful improvement is to prepare well. The more effort you put into ensuring that the foundation for your program is solid, the more time you will save later and the more likely you are to avoid failure.

Planning

Although you might think that "Planning" is interchangeable with "Prepare", there is actually a lot to do before you can produce a plan. I want to make sure you consider options, risks, milestones, etc. and have a written plan for each stage *before you start* any improvement work. In the early stages, that plan can take the form of a few presentation slides explaining what is going to happen, but you must have the following agreed before any work is done:

- Scope.
- Authorized Budget.
- Resources.
- Reporting Mechanisms.

One of the biggest problems Process Improvement initiatives have to face is the conflict with demands on resources for other—sometimes vital—activities. Unless you make sure you plan, then those other activities can—*and will*—soon take precedent and your program will die a quiet but undignified death.

(Appendix B—Improvement Planning gives more advice about planning your program, but you should read that later.)

Preparation Team

In order to implement the changes you want to, you first have to decide what you're going to do and how you're going to do it. That's preparation. Assuming your program is going to have some sort of impact on different groups of people, you also need to prepare for your preparation!

I consider it a pre-requisite that a team of those involved in, or likely to be affected by, the program consider certain issues prior to any "public" kick-off. That means the very first step you have to take is to in effect carry out an impact analysis by answering the PQs in this chapter.

To do this, put together a small—but as representative as possible—team of people. Their objective should be to define the program in its broadest terms; to carry out the groundwork if you will. As a minimum, this group must include one each from the roles, i.e. Policymaker, Manager, Practitioner, and Improver. Somebody needs to be trained in the improvement model(s) you intend to implement, or have some experience in quality management and he or she could act as the team spokesperson.

Having an "outsider", i.e. somebody with no specific team role—to "moderate" meetings will help. You need to make sure this team is as objective and thorough as possible, and an independent hand on the rudder will help steer them towards their goal.

Avoid making this team too management biased. Include a Practitioner or two in the mix. You should try and put your most experienced people into this team, if at all possible, people with experience in other companies or divisions. If you can find experience in Process Improvement (PI) then that's great, but make sure you don't just end up with a PI discussion forum!

The team must report back directly to the top-level management team to an agreed time schedule. Their final report should at least answer all the PQs in this chapter.

So, we have a preliminary Pertinent Question that won't be included in the Responsibility Table:

PQ00—Who should be in our Preparation Team?

Remember—the team's objective is to do the groundwork for your program, not to implement it. The Preparation Team can metamorphose into your top—level Implementation Team (see Appendix C—Implementation Teams) although some "new blood" should always be brought in for implementation.

Teamwork

Of course, one person's failure can be another's route to success, and in large companies there is always going to be somebody benefiting from another's failure. Adapting the CYA Principle[1], one aim should be to make sure that as many rear ends as possible are covered before you start. Your aim must be to ensure that absolutely *nobody's* ass is later exposed to corporate wrath.

You're all in this together. It's not a management thing. It's not a technology thing. It's not a fashion thing. It's the thing which, if you get it right and keep it going right, is going to put you—and keep you—ahead of your competitors.

With improvement programs, it is important to recognize that success has to be measured by all concerned as long term. Benefits have to be recognizable—tangible and measurable—for the customer, for staff, for managers and stockholders. The key phrase is "long term". Although you can grab some "low hanging fruits", the fruits of some improvement measures will only be harvested some time after you have implemented the improvements.

PQ01—How do we build a team (teams) for this program?

PQ02—What skills and resources do we need?

The Consequence of Failure

It might seem an obvious thing to say—that preparation is key to success. In my experience, it's often those obvious things which are forgotten and which make the difference between success and failure.

Once you start, you *mustn't* fail because to do so means not only failure now, but that all your future efforts in this area will be tainted by that failure. It becomes very difficult to put future improvements in place once an improvement program has failed, for whatever reason. You *always* have to make sacrifices in some way to get started and people will be far less willing to make those sacrifices if their perception of its usefulness to them is already colored by a previous failure.

I have endeavored to provide information to help you guard against some of the more common causes of failure for process improvements. The following table summarizes these "failure factors" for each of our roles and you really do need to keep these in mind as your program progresses.

---

1.   Cover Your Ass.

Role	Associated Failure Factor
Policymakers	Setting unrealistic targets and/or arbitrary deadlines.
Managers	Paying lip service instead of providing full support.
Practitioners	Apathy.
Improvers	"Paradigm is all". (Concentrating on the improvement model and not the program.)

If you want to avoid these, and other failure scenarios, then you need to look at the likely risks to your program and how you will deal with them. Do that before they happen rather than after…

PQ03—What are the likely risks to our program?

Program Set-Up

OK, so much for browbeating you about the possible consequences if you don't prepare, what do you actually need to do by way of preparation? Well, the main thing is to do exactly what you would do for *any* project or program, that is, to treat it as a specific and coherent whole with objectives, defined responsibilities, budget, etc.

Your program should have a name.

Try and make it something which won't have people rolling on the floor laughing. Nevertheless, it should be easily remembered and easy to relate to for all. Bear in mind, especially when using an acronym in a multi-national program, that the same word can have different meanings in different languages.

PQ04—How do we incorporate our program into the usual processes?

PQ05—What is the Scope of our program?

PQ06—What should we call our program?

Jump on Passing Bandwagons

If you want to link your program to existing initiatives, well understood long-term business objectives, or make it a sub-set of a wider program, then relationships to those other things need to be defined. It will undoubtedly take time to make such a connection, but it might well be worth it if you can associate your program with an existing success story. Such associations have to be meaningful though, and apparent to everybody, not just some.

Worthwhile link-ups made at the lower levels whose meanings aren't necessarily apparent to policymakers will always be more successful than those which associate one senior management pet with another.

As an example, if you're making a significant investment in your development environment then this might be a good time to introduce your improvement effort. A new development platform, a major technology change, a switch from hardware to software driven functionality; these are all opportunities to have people ask the question "so, what else do we need to change?"

Always take a close look at incoming initiatives of whatever ilk and make sure you evaluate how they will fit to your program and document this so everybody knows. Cling on the shirttails of any successful initiative, just so long as you can show a *meaningful* link.

Even reflected glory will nurture your infant program.

PQ07—How does our program fit to existing initiatives?

PQ08—Is there any synergy or other benefits to be had?

Use Existing Corporate Structures to your Advantage

As much as possible, use existing organization structures and staff.

Introducing a new department to drive improvements is probably not going to work. OK, it might work *eventually*, but not as well as strengthening existing teams with specialist players. Down among your projects, the majority of the improvements will have to be implemented by the Practitioners themselves otherwise they just won't happen. Be careful about bringing outsiders in, although coaching from experts is usually well received as long as those doing the coaching can show some empathy with the staff.

In order to achieve its objectives your improvement program has to be properly funded, resourced and supported. It must be treated just like every other program, using the same planning, budgeting, reporting and accounting procedures.

If taking a top-down approach, defining a corporate program which will cover several levels of the organization, then you must ensure that it is obvious how the different levels interact and what is expected of each. It is not enough to let people figure it out for themselves. On the other hand, you must leave room for some interpretation and creativity in setting up the lower level initiatives.

The "Not Invented Here" syndrome will come into play if you define too much, but failure also beckons if your program lacks co-ordination.

PQ09—How will we fit our program to the organization with maximum benefit and minimum upset?

Inform and Persuade

Once the program is defined, decide how best to support its introduction. If it involves a lot of people (e.g. across a whole company or business unit) then it *will* take longer to prepare.

Although you don't need *everybody's* "buy-in", you do at least need their tacit permission to do it. Involving people from every affected level and part of the organization in the preparation phase will ensure that your program at least survives the Kick-off Meeting.

Be aware of the internal politics likely to affect your program and deal with them in advance. You have to break down the barriers and get people working together in Process Improvement, everybody has to do their bit or you'll soon be out of your depth.

Your program needs to be kicked off properly. This can be seen as part of the preparation, but the truth is that once word is out that this thing exists then you have to inform people about it. If you don't do a proper job of informing staff yourself, then the rumor-mill will do it for you and very quickly jeopardize your success with misinformation, misunderstanding and prejudice.

At the very least, you must take the time to hold Kick-off Meetings at every level and ensure that the program's scope, structure, aims, etc. are communicated and understood. Everyone should be asked to comment and you should not be afraid to change your program to accommodate those needs that you never considered. It certainly helps a lot if people go away from your Kick-off believing that their concerns have been listened to and addressed. They will at least come along for the ride, and that may be as much as you can ask for in the early stages.

PQ10—How do we publicize and institutionalize the program?

Fourth and Inches

Something you can be sure of is that there will be times when your improvement program comes under great pressure. It is important that you have prepared for this. Only you can truly judge what those pressures are likely to be within your organization, but if you're prepared for them, then you can deal with them. (I've tried throughout the book to give examples, but keep your mind W—I—D—E open when considering potential risks.)

Philip Crosby wrote about quality—"Hockey is detection; ballet is prevention". If Process Improvement were a sport, then it would be American Football. And it would always be the last two minutes of the game, six points down, no time-outs left and no John Elway ready to take the field…It's tough, it's a constant pressure, and sometimes it takes courage to stand up and lead.

◆   ◆   ◆

Prepare yourself as best you possibly can—the success of everything that comes later depends on it.

Responsibility Table for PREPARE

Requirement	Policymakers	Managers	Practitioners	Improvers
PQ01—How do we build a team (teams) for this program?	2	5	1	2
Note 1 PQ02—What skills and resources do we need?	2	3	2	3
PQ03—How do we identify and manage risks to our program?	3	4	1	2
Note 2 PQ04—How do we incorporate our program into the usual processes?	4	4	0	2
PQ05—What is the Scope of our program?	5	3	1	1
PQ06—What should we call our program?	2	2	2	4
Note 3 PQ07—How does our program fit to existing initiatives?	3	3	0	4
PQ08—Is there any synergy or other benefits to be had?	3	3	0	4
PQ09—How will we fit our program to the organization with maximum benefit and minimum upset?	4	2	1	3
PQ10—How do we publicize and institutionalize the program?	4	3	1	2

Notes to the Table

Note 1—I believe that responsibility here is split between the operating level of management that allocates resources and the resource user, effectively the Improvers.

Note 2—A management responsibility and one that may well involve different levels, hence the split.

Note 3—Although Practitioners could have some input here, this has to be decided on, and implemented by, management and Improvers.

Quantify

It still amazes me—although I guess it shouldn't by now—just how many projects start off with only a vague idea of how they will know if they succeed. That's to say, without asking and satisfactorily answering *in advance* the question "how will we know if our efforts have been a success?"

Although with most projects we usually know what it is we're trying to achieve—a new software application, a new system, a building complex, an updated configuration—that's not the same as defining up front how you will know when you've achieved it!

There are two main things you need to quantify before you actually start any work on improvements.

- What are our Objectives? *(Why are we doing this?)*
- What are the Success Criteria? *(How will we know if we've succeeded?)*

Objectives

While writing this book, I've headed for the dictionary to confirm my own views on what some words mean. For "objective" my dictionary has lots of those strange phonetic scribblings that only people who write dictionaries understand, but eventually I found the magic words "goal", "aim" and "endeavor".

Regardless of what your own dictionary might say, please accept my definition of an objective as being *something you aim for*. It's what you hope to achieve from your *endeavor*. It's your *goal*.

The quintessence of a meaningful objective is that it should be achievable and measurable. Wishy-washy nonsense like "to be the best in class" or "to be world-class" are best left in the press releases where they belong. You have to define exactly what "best" and "world-class" mean. Go and take a look at your company's Mission Statement and see if it actually has any real meaning. I don't deny that I've seen some that make sense, but many are essentially meaningless and quite rightly get treated as such.

You should try and link your objectives to wider business goals where this makes sense. Giving your improvement program a ride on the back of an existing program perhaps one with wider, but compatible, objectives (for example, reducing Time To Market) will help people to perceive it in their workaday world.

So, remember that *objectives are what you aim to achieve by your endeavors.*

PQ11—Why are we doing this?

PQ12—What can we reasonably expect to achieve?

Success Criteria

However difficult it might be, you have to *plan* for success. It won't just happen by itself. You have to identify what the objectives are, how you will measure whether they've been achieved, and then you have to plan how you're going to make sure you achieve them. These are the things that are the input to your planning—the cornerstone for the program we talked about defining in the previous chapter.

The obvious way of measuring success is to ascertain whether you have reached your objectives. Additionally, there may well be other elements, e.g. risks and benefits that you need to incorporate in your planning for success. In any case, you need to quantify your objectives in a way that can be measured, preferably throughout the program's life and not just at the end.

This is not easy for me to illustrate in general terms, and you need to think hard about what it means for *your* program and then define your Success Criteria in a way which has meaning for everybody involved.

PQ13—How will we identify and measure our success?

Relate to All Levels of the Organization

We already saw that time spent in preparation is not going to be wasted. You need to establish how the different levels of the organization will relate to each other's objectives. Responsibilities for achieving objectives at each level should be clear, but you should leave each individual area of responsibility at those lower levels to define their own way of meeting the overall objectives.

In a Mission Statement, I would probably accept the "best in class" phrase, as long as best in class criteria were explicitly defined for each individual area that was expected to meet the objective. Without that relevance check it remains meaningless.

There have to be objectives and success criteria for every level and for every improvement task. Obviously, the measurements for specific improvement activities will be much more precise than those for the overall program. A reasonable objective for a company-wide program might be "20% reduction in field failures" but that would be meaningless unless it was agreed how that data was to be collected and measured at the lower levels.

PQ14—How can we make sure this reaches all the people we want it to reach? (Refer back to PQ09 and make sure all angles, e.g. management matrices are covered.)

Cost of Quality

Although I've found that the need to reduce costs in development areas is rarely recognized, let alone expedient for those doing the spending, it might help your argument if you can link your program to reducing costs. Although I'm a great believer in the Cost of Quality (or Cost of *Non*-Quality as some organizations call it), I have heard the counter-argument too many times to hold out much hope of being able to use it in earnest in many R&D organizations.

Development units sometimes get "paid" in person years and that system doesn't provide much incentive to reduce costs. "Why should I reduce costs? If I reduce costs, next year I'll get less budget and life's hard enough as it is."

Nevertheless, calculating the Cost of Quality can be a worthwhile tool for concentrating improvement programs, and is without equal for indicating their true worth to the organization. So, if you're able to influence these matters, I would ask you to consider Cost of Quality as an integral part of your improvement program.

You should seek out more information on the subject, but—like all good methods—it is essentially very simple. The idea is that you add together all the costs which go in to assuring quality for your customer and try and reduce them by improving the way you do things, i.e. your processes. This means all those costs, which—in a perfect world where everybody got everything right first time—you wouldn't have to pay.

Some examples of such costs (and the proportion of which might be considered unnecessary) in development areas are:

- Rework (all);

- Problem finding (all except tool/environment issues);
- Problem reporting (all except tool/environment issues);
- Problem solving (all except tool/environment issues);
- Peer Reviews and Document Inspections (some);
- Quality checks (most);
- Testing (most, not all).

I can hear the protestations of testers from here. And I've heard them before…The truth is, that too many good developers are tied up finding other peoples' bugs instead of making their own. Something wrong with that last statement, but you know what I mean and *no* it's not just pie—in—the—sky theory.

Please note that the above list is not exclusive and you need to carefully consider what should go into your own calculations. Virtually all such costs in development relate to time, although there are material costs which should be included, for example, field retro-fits resulting from design faults and test equipment, software licenses, etc. Don't forget associated costs. Field retro—fits doesn't just mean the time your engineers spent getting abused at customer sites—they had to get there too and maybe stay overnight.

What you have to do is to determine which areas of your process, and/or which parts of your organization, are only there because you're not getting it right first time. It is not a coincidence that the quality of systems often hinges on the efficiency of final testing and that for many people "quality" equals "test". Most testing is definitely something which—if you got it right first time—you wouldn't need.

At this point, if you work with software, you might feel the desire to say "oh come on, surely you're not saying we could have fault-free software?!" and yes, I am saying just that. It's because we're prepared to accept second-best when it comes to producing software that "best in class" in software development usually means "making less mistakes". Anyone who has worked for any time in software development knows that fault-free software is theoretically possible, but nobody is going to stake their reputation—or more pointedly, their mortgage—on achieving it. But it remains *possible*.

So, when deciding what costs you should include in your Cost of Quality calculations, you should accept the notion that fault-free products are, theoretically at least, possible. If you don't, then you'll be aiming at achieving *im*perfection, and where's the challenge in that?

The nice thing about the Cost of Quality is that you can gather data quietly, in the background if you have to, and prove its effectiveness before you employ it widely as a tool. There's no harm in collecting data even if you're not convinced about it yourself. Although the initial analysis of what to include should take some time, providing data collection is kept as simple as possible and confined to already available sources, then the rest should be easy.

So what do you actually do with these calculations? Well, the idea is that you try and reduce those costs, usually by targeting a specific area that is hurting you the most and improving the processes used there so that not so many errors are made and costs can be reduced.

You shouldn't restrict yourself to thinking of cost purely in terms of money. As I already said, money might not mean as much to you as time and effort. For you, there may be even more obscure—but meaningful—measures you could adopt. How do you measure the cost to your company's reputation caused by product recalls? Keep your mind open to the possibilities.

The purpose of this book isn't to explain about the Cost of Quality. I merely suggest that you should look at incorporating it into your improvement program as another way of finding out where improvement is needed. In the early days of an improvement program you will often be treating the symptom rather than the disease, and any information you can get to help find root causes will be useful to you in optimizing your efforts and resources.

Sometimes, the catalyst for an improvement program is a significant failure, for example a major retrofit. Although it might be painful—or political—analyzing the costs of that failure can serve as a good primary education in the subject of Process Improvement. You can then compare those costs with that of introducing the improvements that would have avoided the problem.

PQ15—What are the current costs of not getting it right first time?

PQ16—Do we want to use these costs as the focus for our program?

PQ17—If "YES" to PQ16, how do we do that?

Proceed with Caution

Don't set objectives without the agreement of those expected to achieve them. Anyone working in software development in the 1990s will have found it difficult to avoid the Software Engineering Institute's Capability Maturity Model[®1]. The CMM is a way of measuring how good your processes are at producing quality software, i.e. how you guarantee that the customer gets what he wants. There are 5 levels of process "maturity" on the CMM, and most organizations adopting it are trying to reach Level 2, the lowest level being 1 with "ad hoc" processes.

Not unnaturally, corporate improvement programs that implement the CMM tend to make Level 2 an objective for their software development units. This is reasonable enough and—you might think—it would also be reasonable enough to quantify that by adding a deadline, for example, "All software development processes to be at Level 2 by…"

In my humble opinion—or at least in my experience—such simple management statements are probably the source of more PI program failures than any other factor. Unless that goal has been assessed as to whether or not it is achievable, then it will very quickly become a *disincentive* to improvement.

Although we now all have the same goal, there is no consideration taken of the fact that we might not all be in a position to reach that goal. It's the old "if I wanted to get there, I wouldn't start from here" joke. *Where is "here"?*

Has a development unit which has a long way to go at the start but which takes on the challenge, makes sacrifices, works hard and finally doesn't quite achieve the goal *failed*? Has a more mature unit that makes a few adjustments here and there to established processes in order to easily attain the initial goal, but never really recognizes the need for long-term improvement, *succeeded*?

How about the unit developing that vital new product? Are they going to drop that in order to reach CMM[®] Level 2? And if they do, have they succeeded or failed?

Such arbitrary goals simply don't reflect the realities of everyday life, so *please* make sure you don't doom your program before you start through setting unrealistic goals.

◆   ◆   ◆

In summary, **Quantify** means that you need to have some effective way of measuring the success of your program in place before you start.

---

1.   Capability Maturity Model and CMM are registered in the U.S. Patent and Trademark Office by Carnegie Mellon University.

Responsibility Table for QUANTIFY

Requirement ↓	Role → Policymakers	Managers	Practitioners	Improvers
[Note 1] PQ11—Why are we doing this?	3	3	3	1
[Note 2] PQ12—What can we reasonably expect to achieve?	2	2	2	4
PQ13—How will we identify and measure our success?	4	2	2	2
[Note 3] PQ14—How can we make sure this reaches all the people we want it to reach?	3	3	1	3
PQ15—What are the current costs of not getting it right first time?	3	3	0	4
PQ16—Do we want to use these costs as the focus for our program?	4	2	1	3
PQ17—If "YES" to PQ16, how do we do that?	2	3	1	4

Notes to Table

Note 1—Policymakers, Managers and Practitioners can be considered to be the "customers" in this regard and must all say what their expectations are.

Note 2—If the others are the customers for PQ11, then the Improvers must say which of those customer expectations they believe can be realistically achieved. "Reasonable" may not be easily quantifiable but it should be agreed—and documented—what is meant.

Note 3—Although Practitioners can have some input here, agreement is needed from all the others.

Preach Quality

There are lots of people who will tell you what leadership is and how you can get it. Leadership is such an intangible thing to we mere followers, that I don't know if those other people are right or not. What I *do* know is that the number of people who I would happily crawl across broken glass to follow is very small indeed. You either have leadership ability or you don't. Sure, you can learn to act *like* a leader, but you'll likely be found out.

Leader or not, you will have to relate to your colleagues in such a way that they will understand what you're trying to achieve and see that you yourself believe in it.

Because I say so, that's why!

It will certainly help your cause if you're one of those lucky people who can easily carry others along with you. If you're one of the other 99.9%, then you should just be yourself. But…you do have to believe that what you're trying to achieve is right.

Changing peoples' attitudes is never easy and if *you're* not enthusiastic about your program then don't be surprised if other people aren't. If you're not doing it because you really *want* to make it happen, then you probably shouldn't be doing it at all.

If your program is just meant to meet some obscure management objective people won't be fooled. Well, not for long…

In short, you have to mean it!

Honesty is the Best Policy

Be honest about where you are now and where it is you want to go.

Before you can begin to improve, everyone has to recognize the need to improve. If they don't at least *recognize* that need—even if they're not actually persuaded of the need in their own work area—then you won't get much further.

Applying the lessons in the Quantify chapter will help here—you must be able to find suitable data to support your arguments for change.

Have people think about the customer and how their actions impact on the business need of fulfilling the customer's requirements. Encourage them to ask themselves who is the customer for their day-to-day work—not always easy or even seen as relevant for those who never get to see customers. The truth is, that we *all* have customers for our work, even if it's only the person at the next desk.

I think that some of my colleagues through the years have judged me to be crazy. I was long ago persuaded of the argument that prevention is better than cure, so I naturally tend towards an evangelical approach when setting up an improvement project. I've seen the light and I want others to. "OK", they probably think, "he might be crazy but at least he believes in what he's saying".

Real enthusiasm is contagious, pretence is contagion.

PQ18—Are all concerned 100% ready for this?

PQ19—If "NO" to PQ18, what are their doubts/needs and how can they be addressed?

PQ20—Do I promise to tell the truth, the whole truth and nothing but the truth?

As we read in Prepare, to kick off your improvement program you need to be communicating what it is you want to achieve. Part of the communication process is to convince people of your argument. You have to relate your program to *people*, be they practitioner or senior manager. This is not always easy.

Practice your arguments before you deliver them. Tailor your message to suit your audience, senior managers will likely be swayed by other arguments than the Practitioners.

Preaching is very similar to selling—people have to believe that you can deliver on your promises. Just make sure you don't promise what the program can't deliver!

♦   ♦   ♦

As your program progresses, use every little victory over the wicked forces of non-quality to reinforce your arguments. **Preach Quality** at every opportunity and one day you *will* see results.

Responsibility Table for PREACH QUALITY

Requirement / Role	Policymakers	Managers	Practitioners	Improvers
[Note 1] PQ18—Are all concerned 100% ready for this?	4	2	2	2
[Note 2] PQ19—If "NO" to PQ18, what are their doubts/needs and how can they be addressed?	4	1	1	4
[Note 3] PQ20—Do I promise to tell the truth, the whole truth and nothing but the truth?	3	2	2	3

Notes to the Table

[Note 1]—This is effectively a GO/NOGO decision, which must be made by the Policymakers with input and opinion from others.

[Note 2]—Policymakers need to support any required measures, Improvers provide expert advice, and others have input depending on where doubts, resistance, etc. are perceived to be.

[Note 3]—Although everyone has to be prepared to be honest and straightforward in their approach, if the Policymakers and Improvers aren't convincing, then the program will likely fail as people will think there is either an ulterior motive behind the program or that it is just more management bullshit.

Persevere

Philip Crosby wrote in *Quality Is Free* "The time it takes for true, long-lasting, never-to-be-overcome improvement to set in is years. And even then you can never be sure." My own experiences support this. You really do have to work long and hard to get anywhere.

Sometimes you fail.

I have seen more improvement programs fail than I have seen succeed. Not, I assure you, all of my volition! Failure is rarely spectacular. Programs are allowed to wither and eventually die, or are simply ignored until people just don't notice them anymore. Any program which doesn't meet its objectives, be they explicit or merely implied, has failed.

Of all the things in business that you can produce cute theories about, improving quality is probably the only one where the theories outnumber the successes! OK, a slight exaggeration, but never underestimate—especially when the living is easy, the cotton is high and your Momma's good-looking—how tough it really is to see something like this through.

If you follow the "common" Ps and Qs described in these opening chapters, that is, if you put effort and thought into preparing and implementing your program, then your chances of success will be greatly improved, but not *guaranteed*. Everybody has to understand that this is a long-term thing. Yes, you will have defined short-and medium-term objectives, but success is way off in the future, very likely even after you yourself have moved on to something else.

In order to persevere, it's best if you factor into your planning the risks which your program might encounter and prepare for them from the outset, include contingencies for the most likely things in your plan, unless politically expedient not to do so. "The boss is an incompetent fool and must surely get sacked some time soon" might be a valid enough risk, but is probably best left unsaid, or at least unwritten!

There are probably more "*don'ts*" than "*dos*" with regard to ensuring long-term success, and illustrated here are some examples of things which you need to be aware of—*and ready to endure*—in order to ensure the survival of your program.

Think "defense" for a while and figure out where the risks are and how best to avoid them.

Re-organize and Be Damned

The single corporate factor that kills off more improvement programs than any other, is re-organization, rationalization, call it what you will.

From the lower levels of an organization, the workings of senior management can be at best a mystery, at worst totally alien. Sometimes, it's easy to get the feeling that they (policymakers) exist only to impose their own view of the world on the rest of us by coming up with yet another re-organization.

You know the kind of thing—"This realignment of resources will allow us to better focus on the needs of our customers and our shareholders while giving our employees a chance to share in an exciting phase of our corporate development."

Sometimes it makes sense; more often it makes sense only to those privileged few that share the same vision as those charged with turning the company upside down. For people beavering away deep in the bowels of the organization it usually means that, day-to-day, nothing changes except they have to make manual amendments to their business cards before the new ones arrive from the printers.

While *very good* for printers, re-organizations are often *very bad* for improvement programs. Just about every company I've been involved with in recent years has endured a re-organization in the few months I've been with it. Sometimes, the re-organization has been relevant to what I've been trying to achieve in the sphere of improvement, mostly not, but it has *always* had an effect, and that effect has usually been negative.

One organization I was in set up a central, business unit-wide, improvement program complete with full-time Process Improvement staff at all levels. Within a year, the program had been destroyed as the business unit ceased to exist and the Improvers were moved back into development roles. Meanwhile, everyone else worked on the same things as before...At the end, it seemed that only the name of the business unit had changed, but at an enormous and unremarked cost to process quality and to Improver morale.

In a nutshell, set up your program in such a way that at best, it can operate independently of business units and other corporate entities; at worst, so that it can't be lost just because of name changes. (This really goes for all levels, but the greatest effects usually originate from on high.)

PQ21—How independent can our program be without becoming an orphan?

PQ22—What mechanisms can we use to ensure that our program will always be considered and not just killed during a re-organization?

Let The Dust Settle

Just as you must persevere with your program when re-organizations come along, so it has to endure staff changes. New brooms, for such is the nature of brooms, inevitably try to sweep clean. They need to be persuaded that, yes, while some things are best swept away, your improvement program isn't one of them.

Although such programs will inevitably depend for their success on the motivation and enthusiasm of those involved—just like any other corporate venture—they will also have to endure personnel changes during their lifetime. This is because improvement programs last for years, not weeks or months, and their success can only really be measured after any improvements have been successfully piloted. (That usually means seeing more than one complete project through using the improved process.)

Try and include targets related to the improvement program in peoples' appraisals. Have specific roles and responsibilities written into job descriptions. Make the program survive because it's in everyone's interests for it to do so.

Stock Prices Can Go Down As Well As Up

Not that anyone believes it of their own portfolio of course…You have to understand that you are going to see bad times as well as good during the life of your improvement program.

In the early stages, things can often seem to be going very badly, but you have to stick with it. In fact, programs which start badly, and so are forced to overcome problems with perception, commitment and politics from the outset are more likely to succeed than those which fail to address, or even recognize, such problems.

Your program, its staff and sponsors need to be resilient enough to resist pressures to fail and all must recognize in advance that problems *will* occur. Likely risks should be outlined in advance in the program's planning and tracked throughout its life, with new risks being analyzed and tracked as they arise. Don't expect plain sailing, and at least be prepared for the possibility of rough seas ahead!

PQ23—How will we identify and manage risks which arise during the life of the program?

Money Makes the World Go Around

No improvement program should ever fail because of lack of money or resource.

If you're meeting your objectives, then it should be easy to track and prove the program's efficiency. If you are unable to show any improvement, then don't be surprised if corporate finance provides plenty of good reasons to use the corporate axe…

Always be ready to compromise. Any improvement is better than none, if the money's not available for everything you need to do, well, it will just take you longer, that's all.

◆   ◆   ◆

Two more "Ps" spring out when we talk about the need to **Persevere**, namely "perpetuate" and "permanence". Do whatever it takes to avoid the inevitable corporate hurdles, which your program will encounter en route, but whatever happens, **DON'T QUIT!**

Responsibility Table for PERSEVERE

Requirement	Policymakers	Managers	Practitioners	Improvers
PQ21—How independent can our program be without becoming an orphan?	3	3	2	2
PQ22—What mechanisms can we use to ensure that our program will always be considered and not just killed during a re-organization?	4	4	1	1
[Note 1] PQ23—How will we identify and manage risks which arise during the life of the program?	3	3	1	3

Note to the Table

[Note 1]—Refer back to PQ03 and make sure your risk management isn't confined to a one—off analysis.

People

I slid into software development by accident, not design, having previously stood outside the software department gazing in with awe and a shocked expression. Anyone who has worked *with* software development rather than *inside it,* will know what I mean. Just as the concept of software doesn't fit easily with our physical world, so the world that software developers inhabit can appear quite odd to those on the outside looking in.

The view from the inside looking out is sometimes just as bewildering, and I've spent a lot of time trying to facilitate communications between technical areas and those with which they interface. Such links can be key to the success of product development, especially when identifying, gathering and allocating requirements—a "traditional" weakness in bringing new technology to market.

There is a kind of Bermuda Triangle nebula surrounding technical areas in which the dictates of policymakers take on an otherworldly aspect or simply disappear without trace.

◆　　　◆　　　◆

Of Beards & Sandals

Engineers, even software engineers, are human. Despite the overwhelming evidence to the contrary. OK, in some cases it might take complex DNA tests to establish the fact, but engineers *are* human.

Make no mistake, the real power in technical areas—although this probably goes more for software than other areas—lies with the Practitioners themselves. It is they who decide what will be done and how it will be done. Although some managers try and tell themselves otherwise, this is the way it really is.

So, when and if you want to change something in the way you meet your customer's requirements, these are the people who have to make it happen. If they don't want the improvement program to succeed, then it won't.

Perception

The way we perceive things is colored by our prejudice and opinion formed by our experiences. Our perception affects the way we communicate with other people.

Communications between those charged with facilitating or implementing improvements have to be effective. One of the keys to this is to never make assumptions that what you're hearing is what is being said and vice versa. Doubts must be voiced, brows furrowed and questions asked before you can make even the simple assumption that you're all talking the same language.

Computer people use common words in familiar but tangential ways. Some are deadly earnest about, well, *everything*. Worse, not only do they laugh at Dilbert cartoons because they're true, they readily accept that dogs might run companies. If there isn't actually anything in the currently flavor-of-the-decade programming language to preclude it happening, then it must be possible.

This is a question of perception and everyone has to recognize that different views exist and have to be accommodated.

Specifically, non-technical people must not feel they have to pretend they understand something that they actually don't. Technical people must make every effort to make themselves understood by using non-technical terminology. This is a challenge for everybody, but one that needs to be accepted, and a fight that has to be won. Glossaries of terms, standard use of abbreviations and careful use of narrative descriptions will all help, but most of all everyone has to recognize the need to communicate more effectively.

Over the years, the IT community has bastardized so many common words that sometimes it can be quite unnerving. Necessarily, acronyms abound and, having worked in several companies, I can tell you that the same few letters can have quite different meanings, sometimes even between different projects in the same organization.

For any technical improvement program to succeed, everyone involved has to work hard at making themselves understood and at understanding others. It is too easy to ignore the differences that exist, or to try and bridge them by artificial means. The efficiency of your processes, and thereby the quality of your product, depend to a great deal on ensuring that simple, effective, communications exist and are supported by all concerned.

Why Can't You Understand? It's Simple Enough!

Assumptions are the most potent enemy of effective communication.

Because we all perceive things differently, and process information from our own unique viewpoint, we readily assume that others understand what we are saying. And they do. But, they understand it from *their* own unique viewpoint, which could be quite different from our own.

Happily, I learned this lesson quite early in my Process Improvement career. I was discussing process issues with a group of what were then called "programmers" and—for reasons lost in the mists of time and probably best forgotten—we had to define what was meant by the phrase "a software module".

"That's easy," said one "it's a unit of code providing specific functionality that can't be sub-divided" and he sat back with a self-satisfied smile.

"No no" chipped in another, "it's two or more units of code which together blah blah".

Well, OK, he never actually said "blah blah" but he might as well have done. The fact was that both would happily converse about this or that "software module", assuming they were talking about the same thing. In fact, they were talking about different things.

The old adage—"Assume makes an ASS out of U and ME" is as true today as it's ever been.

Process Improvement is 90% People and only 10% Process

Always remember that when you are talking about Process Improvement you are talking about *people* changing the way things get done. Yes, there are tools, development environments, programming languages and many ways of realizing the developed technologies, but all of these depend upon *people* for their successful implementation.

Improvement success is achieved by and through people, not a process handbook. Like any human endeavor, the nearest you can get to a guarantee of success is to pick the right people.

Implementation Teams

As we saw earlier, the composition of your Preparation Team is very important. I have split the roles of preparation and implementation teams although you could use the same people for both. I would always recommend bringing in some new blood for the implementation phase of your program. The people being replaced will be able to go back and support understanding and implementation of the program within their usual work groups. This approach of revitalizing teams will greatly help in the business of promoting the program by increasing familiarity with it.

The number and composition of your implementation teams will depend on the size and scope of your program and organization, but their objective is always the same—to support the implementation of Process Improvement within a specified area of responsibility. At the higher levels, the key word is "support"—actual improvement of processes is the role of the implementation teams of Practitioners and Improvers.

Implementation Teams facilitate improvement work. They steer the program within their defined area by making sure that resources are available, risks are identified, problems solved or escalated and so on.

At the higher levels—probably down to location or independent unit—the role of implementation teams will tend towards the administrative. At lower levels each planned improvement activity should have its own implementation team whose job it is to analyze the current process, find improvement opportunities, run workshops, write process descriptions, etc.

Exactly how implementation teams will work will depend on how you choose to set them up. I wouldn't want to restrict you in how you approach this. I would, however, always strive for a high degree of connectability across teams. For example, somebody sitting in a unit team could also be that unit's representative on the higher level team.

Your organization may already be using "Quality Circles" or similar. The way they work may or may not be defined. If it is, try and use what exists, but ensure you include all the elements for implementation teams described here and later. If it isn't described, then pilot the implementation team approach, make sure it works and then take it out into other areas for use by quality circles (and maybe gain some kudos as a result).

You will find more about the work of improvement teams in Appendix C—Implementation Teams, in the meantime consider the following PQs.

PQ24—How many levels of implementation will we have?

PQ25—How will we resource our teams?

◆   ◆   ◆

More than ever, and more than we like to admit in technical areas, **People** are the key to success. Everybody has their part to play in realizing this success and as well as the common factors described in the previous chapters, there are things that are specific to certain *people*. Most of the remainder of this book is therefore divided into four main parts reflecting the roles I identified in the chapter "Ps And Qs?" *viz.*:

- Policymakers' Part, which is aimed primarily at senior management or "Policymakers".

- Manages' Part, which is aimed at line and project managers.

- Practitioners' Part, which is aimed at staff (development and operative) of all levels and types.

- Improvers' Part, which is aimed at anyone actively involved in supporting or driving through the implementation of improvements.

This doesn't mean that you shouldn't read all the chapters, indeed you should assuming that you've paid for the privilege. My experience has shown me that although everybody has to be headed in the same direction when it comes to striving for improvement, different people take different routes to get there.

Responsibility Table for PEOPLE

Requirement ↓	Role → Policymakers	Managers	Practitioners	Improvers
[Note 1] PQ24—How many levels of implementation will we have?	3	3	1	3
[Note 2] PQ25—How will we resource our teams?	3	4	1	2

Notes to the Table

Note 1—You *will* have different levels. Even the smallest program should have one group "steering" and facilitating, with another taking care of the nitty-gritty of improvement activity. You might need to structure your teams around a matrix management or multiple product lines. Make sure the teams fit the organization, but remember to give them as much independence as possible from the effects of re—organizations and politicking.

Note 2—Will you only use volunteers? Punishment detail? Drag people in off the street? In all seriousness, give it some thought—it might not be as easy you think! Relate success in PI to career plans—make participation an incentive rather than a chore.

Policymakers' Part

This section of the book is aimed at what is loosely termed "Senior Management". I've used the term "Policymakers", because I mean whoever holds the purse strings and can grant a "yay" or "nay" to the wishes of others—those people who set the business objectives. In multinationals, this can be at corporate or business unit level, for smaller organizations it will usually be "The Boss".

Dependent upon corporate culture, it might also be the head of a particular development unit enjoying autonomy because of location or simply because nobody else in the organization knows what the heck it is those people do. So, Policymakers need not necessarily be "senior managers", they just most likely will be.

A crucial part of this book's *raison d'être* is the premise that there are certain roles that are important when considering Process Improvement; and that of the Policymaker is indeed crucial to success or failure. More than one improvement program that I have encountered has been doomed at conception because of a lack of understanding by Policymakers (albeit well meaning), about how their directives will be received.

You will recall from an earlier chapter, a few words of caution when setting objectives and of the company I know which declared that all software development areas would reach Level 2 on the CMM® by a certain deadline. This deadline was set with virtually no input from the development staff who would have to make it happen.

No surprise then, that it simply didn't happen.

A senior developer told me—with the frankness which only those secure in their jobs can—that he had no intention of helping to achieve that goal because the rumor-mill had it that his manager would get a bonus if he did. Yes, there was a need for better processes, but why should he work his butt off working late just so his boss could get a bonus?

The target wasn't reached, management credibility suffered and—worst of all—Process Improvement was seen by the Practitioners as a joke and as something that could safely be ignored.

If you are one of the people who are paid for making decisions or defining policy within your organization you have to be aware of certain realities which the people around you might just not tell you.

Whatever your corporate culture, no matter how many times you "meet the troops" or go on presidential-style walkabouts on your travels, you are most definitely not in tune with "the workers" (which includes development staff). This is regardless of how nice a person you are or how well practiced your leadership skills; it's simply a case of perspective.

There are some obvious reasons for this, as well as some which will be specific to you as an individual or to your company. You inhabit a different world to them. Even if you remain convinced that you are in perfect accord with your organization, then you will hopefully at least accept that your perspective is different.

Efficient—and effective—communications is one of the keys to success and that desire to communicate has to start at the top.

Some companies have regular ways of communicating between Policymakers and everyone else, but even there you encounter the question of perception. Your perception (even if you started at the bottom and worked your way up) is going to be different. The things you deal with on a day-to-day basis are on a quite different scale, and your motivation different from the people who build the quality into the products and services on which your company's future depends.

Whatever your personal style, the fact is that from your lofty retreat, high above the peasantry you necessarily see THE BIG PICTURE. The people around you see THE BIG PICTURE.

In order to form the basis for success, however, THE BIG PICTURE has to relate to all the little pictures from which it is made up. And it's where those little pictures join that THE BIG PICTURE is most likely to break up.

Consider the following "Ps and Qs" and how best to apply them to your own organization and so ensure that THE BIG PICTURE fits with the little pictures…

PICK

You have to make sure the right people are involved. That means not just ensuring that the program is properly staffed, but also supporting it in areas where only you can exert the required influence. For example, there may well be problems in gathering customer requirements that can only be addressed by involving marketing people and/or customers.

It's your job to open the doors to those departments that interface to the areas your program seeks to address.

Typically, this will mean at least assigning a *pro-active* liaison person from each department which has impact on—or is impacted by—the process areas being addressed. For example, you might well find that the failure of processes within development are causing problems elsewhere, in which case those people will be happy to get involved. Most likely areas would be Marketing, Customer Service and Production. (Not untypical, is that these functions also cause problems for development and so your diplomatic skills will be put to the test.)

Think carefully about who needs to be involved and keep your mind wide open while you do it.

As Program Sponsor, pick someone from your own team who has a thorough knowledge of—and experience in—the areas you hope to improve.

Somebody who knows how to guide others rather than leading by example—diplomacy, empathy and political *nous* will be needed to guide your fledgling program into the corporate consciousness. You will only add to your problems if the sponsor's main interest is in rolling up metaphorical sleeves and getting things done before they're ready to be done.

Patience and persistence are the keys to successful sponsorship.

"OK", you might say, "I'll ask the experts—we have corporate quality people, let them do it." Remember that your corporate quality department, like you, sees THE BIG PICTURE. Typically, they will set up a nice intranet site, they will produce pretty documents with great names like "Corporate Quality Manual", they will have you sign laudably plausible quality policies and they will do a fine job of entertaining auditors. Unfortunately, the chances are that they will have as much credibility with Practitioners as last year's technology.

That's not to say that corporate quality doesn't have a role to play, but that role should be defined by the organization's perception of them. Make them central to the success of your Process Improvement program and you will probably just add to your problems.

Rarely, I should say in all honesty *very* rarely, have I encountered a corporate quality function that could actually contribute positively to such efforts from the outset. If you're convinced of the need to improve quality then it stands to reason that, with the best will in the world, existing quality functions aren't working as you would like.

It's not their fault your processes don't work, but their job *ought* to be making sure those processes *do* work. Chances are, they've probably just got the same disease as the rest of the organization!

There may well be individuals within your corporate quality organization who can help in the implementation of your program, certainly it is there that you should look for expertise in whatever model(s) you are trying to implement. These people should mentor your Improvers. (By all means bring in outside help, but the thrust has to come from within the areas to be improved, otherwise its likelihood of success will be weakened.)

For more on the role of Quality and other support staff, see Never Mind The Quality—Feel The Width.

Picking the actual resources to be your Improvers will most likely be done by your managers (and I have included "PICK" there too), but you need to be active in your support for this process.

PQ26—How can I make sure the right people are involved?

PATIENCE

As already discussed, if you make realistic objectives that can be reached, it stands to reason that you're going to have to be patient if you are to reach your overall improvement objectives. Probably more patient than you might want…

Learn from past mistakes, don't let the program fail just because a few objectives aren't reached.

Softly softly catchee monkey…

PQ27—What happened to those previous programs that fell within our definition of "Process Improvement"?

PROGRESS

Measure progress through regular reports. Mostly, I encourage people to use existing channels and structures for what they do, but I would suggest you consider cutting the red tape and receive reports directly from your top-level implementation team rather than having it filtered by the Program Sponsor or "usual channels".

This makes the Improvers feel wanted. It also shows to the rest of the organization that you see this as important. Have the Improvers report direct to you, e.g. by making a progress presentation to your regular management team meeting each month, rather than having the Program Sponsor do it.

Honesty is key—the Improvers have to feel that you're listening to them and you have to react on what they say. Part of this is your saying in advance what information you require rather than waiting for them to tell you. Obviously, there might be a need for some discussion as to exactly what will be reported, but you must take the lead. The sources and validity of data available will probably be limited, so be prepared to compromise!

PQ28—What do I want to have reported to me, how and when?

PROMOTE

Take every opportunity—without falling into the insincerity trap—to raise the profile of the program. You must support it constantly, and particularly every time it hits a problem.

Don't just support it, *promote* it. Rather than providing a crutch when it starts to limp, make sure it's kept in tip-top condition all the way. Make it YOUR baby rather than farming it out to the corporate nursemaids…

PROFIT

This is somewhere that your BIG PICTURE perception is an asset. You insist on knowing the effect on the bottom line for everything else—make sure somebody works out a way that you can see it for your improvement program too.

Initially, the effect might well be negative cost-wise, but if you prepare and plan properly then you should know that in advance. I would avoid setting cost-related targets in development Process Improvement too early, but you should gather that data from the outset so that you will have a basis for future decisions on where to make improvements.

PRUDENCE

A curious word this to find in a business book. The idea that you should take care to consider yourself (i.e. CYA) might seem at odds with what I've had to say so far. But, it is important that you ensure that the playing field you're defining is leveled for everybody, yourself included.

Define realistic and obtainable objectives for the top level of your program. Don't dictate arbitrary deadlines before you have a basis for knowing whether they're achievable. That means you must first properly evaluate the current position before deciding what needs to be done in order to reach the target.

In avoiding the errors most often attributed to senior managers you must take care to not go too far in the other direction and tie your program up in red tape!

Be sure to make sure…

PQ29—Are my pants fireproof?

QUALIFY

OK, OK…I admit to having pored over the dictionary for this one! Here we're talking about "qualify" in the sense of helping people prepare themselves for the job in hand.

You have to make sure that people are empowered to achieve what you expect of them. That means:

- Do they have the right skills?
- Do they have the right training?
- Do their managers support them?

PQ30—What do I still need to do to empower the people who have to implement the improvements and to ensure they will be supported as the program progresses?

POLITICS

Every organization has internal politics. You have to cut through them. Improvers must be able to work free of unnecessary hindrance, this means that you have to at least gain your peers' and subordinates' acceptance for the program. If they see you supporting it and you set it up right, then their support and active involvement will follow.

I was once involved in a major improvement program which had been set up in such a way that the group charged with driving the improvements through were independent of the areas which had to be improved. This was an old established company[1] with a rigid, patriarchic management hierarchy. From a certain level and up, managers had absolute power over their people. Not life and death, you understand (at least I never heard of any executions while I was there) but what they said went for their area and that was it. Very little discussion and certainly no arguments...

The Improvers came from within the company and so shared that mind-set. They devised a centralized improvement function. And then they organized meetings. Endless meetings, an example of which was the weekly steering group meeting which just about everybody attended. The external consultants were there, the Improvers were there, and representatives from the target departments were there. The catering bill must have been enormous—enough cookies were consumed to affect the price of wheat.

I came to refer to this body as the "Politburo" and those of us charged with driving through improvements did so in spite of the improvement program, rather than because of it. Those department heads that didn't want to play simply ignored the whole thing, paying lip-service as necessary for the sake of appearance. The whole thing struggled on—probably struggles on still—but it was doomed as an effective tool from the outset. The bureaucratic approach added to the problem rather than addressing it.

By succumbing to politics the Improvers doomed their program to having no credibility, no bite and no chance...

Only *you* can gauge how politics and culture will affect the program within your own organization, all I will say is that they can kill it if you don't address such issues before you start.

PURPOSEFUL

Be it.

---

1. And no, the company concerned isn't mentioned in the Bio on the cover. I'm trying to forget them and they've certainly forgotten me...

◆   ◆   ◆

To summarize, it's your role to define a working structure for your program that utilizes existing corporate structures but which takes into account the different perspectives of the various players. There has to be a link between top and bottom that can be followed through the various layers without being lost.

You need to take the time and trouble to ensure that your program isn't built on the shifting sands of corporate whim. That means applying the Ps and Qs you've already read about (PREPARE, QUANTIFY, PREACH QUALITY, PERSEVERE, PEOPLE) to your area of influence, as well as the specific factors outlined above.

Responsibility Table for POLICYMAKERS

Requirement	Policymakers	Managers	Practitioners	Improvers
[Note 1] PQ26—How can I make sure the right people are involved?	10			
[Note 2] PQ27—What happened to those previous programs that fell within our definition of "Process Improvement"?	10			
PQ28—What do I want to have reported to me, how and when?	10			
[Note 3] PQ29—Are my pants fireproof?	10			
PQ30—What do I still need to do to empower the people who have to implement the improvements and to ensure they will be supported as the program progresses?	10			

Notes to the Table

Note 1—Refer back to the Prepare chapter and make sure that your influence is felt in answering the PQs you find there.

Note 2—Take an honest look at your organization's prior record and ask yourself what lessons you should take from previous failures (or successes—no matter how limited).

Note 3—Check the zipper too—you wouldn't want it to jam if your pants were on fire.

Managers' Part

How do you lead, or deal with, technical development staff without turning into Dilbert's pointy-haired manager? Well, a good start is not to ban Dilbert cartoons from the office. I could write a book about managing technical development, but it would all boil down to "it ain't easy is it?" I will confine myself here to the matter in hand, although I do have a couple of things to say on the subject of management intended to help the success of your program.

Many of the problems one encounters with technical development are the result of simple breakdowns in communication.

If I want a house built, all I have to understand is what I want to see at the end of the project; I have to put my trust in the experts to do their job. Just as I can get an insight into how work on my house is progressing by taking a look every now and then, so I can look at technical development and see how it's going. I just need to know what to look for. I believe it helps when managers concentrate on managing and allow their staff to get on with whatever it is they do. That goes for improvement work too.

What do I mean by "manager"? Many organizations differentiate between functional and project—sometimes *product*—organizations. My intended audience here is anyone who has a primary role in the allocation and administration of resources. In other words, are you the one who decides who does what and where?

I have deliberately not dealt with project managers as a separate group. Project managers/leaders who request resources of the line organization and assign them to specific tasks have a foot in both camps and need to consider equally the Practitioners' Part as well as this chapter. Because it's difficult to completely avoid using the term "manager" generically, I haven't capitalized it in the same way as I have the other roles.

◆　　◆　　◆

Being a manager, anything with the word "Quality" and/or "Improvement" in the title has proved to be a right royal pain in the butt for you in the past hasn't it? It means taking people off development projects to fiddle around until the next project crisis. Then, everything gets back to normal while the so-called "improvement" activities slowly, but surely, slide first on to the back burner and then down the back of the stove.

What a waste of time and resource!

Believe me when I say I have sympathy with your plight. It takes a lot of faith to do what you *have to do* in order for the improvement program to succeed. In your role you are both key to success and one of the biggest potential contributors to failure. I shall assume that you are at least prepared to do the best job you can given your circumstances. Look, nobody ever said to me "OK, Dave—take as many people as you want to get this improvement stuff done". I've heard all the sob—stories before, so spare me…

You should particularly acquaint yourself with the Prepare chapter earlier in the book and consider how you can make those things happen in your own area of influence. There are some other Ps and Qs which you also need to bear in mind in your quest to merge the needs of the improvement program into your overall planning.

PRIORITISE

People need to know how important this is. Say so, precisely and without room for misunderstanding—"Project X is Priority 1, then comes Process Improvement work, then everything else".

You should be doing that anyway where different projects utilize the same resources. If not, then maybe your project management processes need improving…

Review the priorities on a regular basis—you might like to shift the improvement activities to the top in "slack" periods for example. What?! You don't have "slack"?! You need to start an improvement program…

Juggling the needs of different projects and the pressure from different quarters is never easy, but at least if you do it on a regular basis using the same criteria, everyone can see how it's done and they all know how important this stuff is to you. Or not. You decide…

PQ31—How high a priority can we assign to this work?

PROJECT

Having decided how to relate the overall program to your local environment and prioritized according to the overall development needs, you can now define your own improvement project(s). Just to clarify—here, I'm using the term "program" to describe the overall effort and "project" for the various lower-level initiatives. I'm assuming that managers will be responsible for setting up and supporting one or more of those projects.

You should make sure that the improvement project is defined, planned, tracked and reported on in exactly the same way as every other project you have. Only if you do this, can you expect to be able to make judgments about it by way of comparison with other projects. You need to have the same objective view that your planning and tracking system hopefully gives you, to allow you to know which projects are doing well and which not. If you don't have such a planning and tracking system, then use the improvement project itself as a pilot for such a process. (Always try using the improvement project as a pilot where it's feasible to do so—it can work well.)

Insist on being told, on a regular basis, what progress has been made against the objectives set, make sure resources are being used properly and that the information you get from the project is what you need to be able to report to your own management. Your role here as a link between the bottom and the top is just as important as in any of your other activities.

Make your improvement project into a "real" project and it will be far more likely to succeed than if you treat it as an administrative overhead.

PICK

It's often very easy to judge whether management is committed to an improvement program by the quality of the resources they assign to it.

Some improvement models are more specific about this than others, but I would say it stands to reason that if you are striving to get things better then you need to set your best people to work on the problem. My reasoning is as follows.

The existence of an improvement program indicates that the organization has recognized the need to improve, *ergo,* is doing something "wrong". Perhaps "wrong" has become your norm, and the implication is that if you could get it "right" by ordinary means then you probably would already. So, to get it "right" means you have to make an *extra*ordinary effort. That means putting your best people to work on it for as much of their time as can be spared.

There are advantages for you as a manager in this approach. Project resources are scarce. If you accept that some of that precious resource is spent on activities—re-work, review, problem solving—which might be avoided with the application of better processes, then any effort you put into improving those processes will give a payback in effort saved on your projects.

View improvements as a key activity in optimizing your resource usage and it becomes easier—expedient even—to assign high quality resources to it. So, pick your best people to work on these things. Usually, that will mean people with the most experience.

"Best" here also means the right combination of experience of the organization, its products and the processes used to achieve them, together with a certain personal *cachet*. It is important that the people you choose to implement your improvement program can relate to the rest of the development staff. That also ensures they will be listened to.

The Improvers have to be acceptable as people who are worth listening to, purely because they share the same day-to-day pressures and problems of the Practitioners. Don't just take volunteers though. The enthusiasm you want in your program needs to be offset by the cynicism of people who have "been there, done that, worn the T-shirt to death". Make sure great care is taken in choosing your Improvers group.

There are other factors to consider as well, such as the suitability of those people to do the job. Take a look at the Ps & Qs in the chapter Improvers' Part and you will recognize that the personal attributes needed to achieve these are not universal.

Set a thief to catch a thief…

PQ32—Who will get the job done?

PLEDGE

Your support. Sign up to support concrete objectives, not some wishy-washy "best in class" mission statement. (You might be thinking by now that I have a "thing" about mission statements. You might be right.)

You need to fit the objectives of the overall improvement program to the various local factors that are affected by it. Think about what it means to the development projects, the line organization, peoples' objectives, and your own targets.

Write it down and sign it. If others see *you* signing up to specific, measurable, improvement targets then they might start to think there's something to this project in spite of any doubts they may have.

Signing up to concrete objectives should be done at all levels, but is most important closest to the Practitioners. They have to believe that this is something that will be wholeheartedly supported or they won't waste their time doing it. They have enough pressure as it is, they probably have workarounds for the most recurrent problems, so why should they waste their time trying to change things? *Because you are making it happen, that's why, and not just because you say so.*

PROTECT

Your improvement project will be under attack from all sides through much of its life. You have to anticipate this.

It is the nature of organizations with the greatest need for improvement that any activity which doesn't directly add to the required output will be at best ignored, at worst actively discouraged.

This is because everyone has to work that much harder to get things done due to the effects of their poor processes. It's not because people set out deliberately to undermine an improvement effort, that's just sometimes the result.

If you're convinced of the validity of the improvement project, then you must use all your management and political skills to avoid and combat attacks on it. Where all else fails, you have to put your back to the wall and defend it with whatever comes to hand!

Don't give yourself the option of quitting. If you simply can't allow your people to spend any time on improvement activities, then delay them. Just make sure they aren't forgotten, and that a review of the original plan is scheduled for whenever the latest crisis is over and you can start improvement work again.

PARTICIPATE

Be active.

Maybe you were once a Practitioner yourself? Think back and consider what you would have thought about this improvement stuff and make sure that you get involved in discussing the fears, doubts, defiance, which people will show (if you're lucky) or harbor if you're not).

Certainly, you must make sure that the Improvers have access to you. This is best done through regular progress meetings, but those managers who take the time to get involved with the project will see the quickest improvements. A word of warning—there is a thin line between being involved and being a pain in the butt.

PQ33—Where can I get involved and add some value?

PRAISE

But only where praise is due.

Responsibility Table for MANAGERS

Requirement → Role	Policymakers	Managers	Practitioners	Improvers
Note 1 PQ31—How high a priority can we assign to this work?		10		
Note 2 PQ32—Who will get the job done?		10		
Note 3 PQ33—Where can I get involved and add some value?		10		

Notes to the Table

Note 1—Be realistic, but remember your commitment will be reflected in your answer. Consider also your ability to stick with your decision when the going gets tough later in the program.

Note 2—Not "who can we spare?" That should be a supplementary question to this and not an alternative!

Note 3—If the answer is "I can't" for any reason, then confine yourself to an administrative, supportive role. Managers who arrive late or re—arrange PI meetings to suit their own schedules do not help.

Practitioners' Part

I have tried, in the earlier chapters to describe how the groundwork for a successful improvement initiative can be laid. This chapter is aimed at the group of people who can actually make or break the improvement effort—Practitioners.

Yes, the decisions of managers do have an effect, but they can't actually *do it*, nor can the Improvers. In order to improve the way you do things, the people who have to implement those improvements are the ones involved in doing the work.

This might sound obvious, but too often Practitioners are treated like extras in a film rather than as central to the plot. To clarify, by "Practitioners" I mean everyone concerned with realizing whatever it is you provide as well as the people providing them with support. In development areas, we're not just talking about software or hardware engineers—there are plenty of potential process pitfalls before they even get involved. Rather, I mean everybody whose activities have a direct effect on the final product or service, which means not just "techies" but support and administrative staff of one sort or another. (You will find more on this in the section Never Mind The Quality—Feel The Width.)

The pressures on development organizations haven't changed very much in the years I've been working in them. It's the same old thing—there are never enough skilled people. No, resources aren't the only problem facing technical development, but whatever the pressures that are brought to bear by demanding customers, shortened time-to-market cycles and new technology, they manifest themselves in the form of too few people trying to do too much with too little time. No wonder then, that improvement programs sometimes fail in the very areas they are intended to help—people simply don't have the time to spend on things with no obvious immediate payback.

Of course, this provides a neat excuse for Practitioners, and I could have been a rich man if only I had charged for listening to the "we'd like to, but this is the *real* world" mantra. (I realize that people don't use the resource excuse without valid reason. Developers are the front-line troops of technology, any technology. Researchers, marketers, sales, production, you name them—*nobody* has quite the same constant time pressures Which developers.)

I have a lot of sympathy for developers who often find themselves working to realize other peoples' half-baked ideas to unfeasible deadlines. More time is wasted on projects before technical specification than in any other phase. Ideas are kicked around for months or years before R & D are ordered to get the thing ready by some arbitrary deadline.

There's not a lot R & D can do about this, except maybe avoid adding to their problems by pussyfooting around with cute process stuff. OK, what if you *do* improve your processes to the point where you're saving time, they'd only give you even stricter deadlines, so why bother?

◆   ◆   ◆

There are two things that anyone has to believe in before they will start improving the way they work—

- That there is a good reason for doing so.
- That they will see some benefit from it.

Otherwise, what is the point?

Apart from those naïve souls fresh from training, Practitioners have seen it all before. Despite the cynicism which the failure of previous programs may have left, let us assume that the improvement program has been launched in your area and you're going to have to do something.

You could use the tried and tested "ignore it for long enough and it will go away" ploy. Or you can try, as a first step, to answer these important questions for yourself—

PQ34—What is my motivation for doing this?

PQ35—What benefits will I see from it?"

Re-read the Preface and then ask yourself whether you too, being human, might therefore be imperfect enough to make mistakes.

PURSUE PERFECTION

Of course, you know that you make mistakes, but are you *really* delivering the best quality that you can, or simply what the customer will accept?

Is your product already "good enough"? Ask your customer, and if you get the feeling that maybe that's all your stuff is—"good enough" then you really need to ask yourself do I want to be "good enough" or do I want to be the best?

Some people enjoy finding errors and solving problems. Dare to be different—enjoy not making errors in the first place!

What is actually possible in *your* development environment? Don't restrict yourself to the horizons defined by your previous experience—you must try and leave those behind. Be honest with yourself and don't avoid facing up to problems just because you don't see any easy way to solve them.

One of the most common things I find is that, rather than take the time and trouble to work through and solve a problem, people will take steps to avoid it, work around it or simply pretend it doesn't exist. Problems *are* going to occur, and you have to tackle them before you can go forward.

Face up to process problems, don't be pushed around by them!

QUESTION

As well as questioning yourself, question others. Question your boss, question the company, and question every single thing that stops you from reaching the perfection you seek. Ask awkward questions and insist on honest answers. Everybody has their part to play and although we naturally tend to see others' mistakes and not our own, so everyone needs to be made aware that they are causing problems for others.

You included...

Be warned that when asking those questions you need to be prepared to help find the answers, and that sometimes you might need to wait till the right moment.

But, never stop questioning. Nothing kills off an improvement program better than apathy. It's a slow death, but it's a sure one...

POSSIBILITIES

Just before you go off and become a total pain in everyone else's butt by asking all those uncomfortable questions, you need to consider what can be realistically achieved. Remember, the purpose of this isn't to make your life any harder, or easier, it's to improve quality. It's to give your customers what they want...

You already know those areas that are ripe for improvement, don't you? Consider the following for a moment.

PQ36—Where do I have the most problems?

PQ37—Where do I "make do and mend" in my processes?

PQ38—Where do I have to circumvent "the system" because the system's too damn slow or simply doesn't work?

PQ39—Where am I "getting away with it"?

Provide the answers to these questions and you are spotting improvement opportunities, some of which will benefit you as well as—ultimately—your customer.

POSITIVE

If you're "against" the improvement program, ask yourself why. Are you actually against it or are you just cynical because of past experience or hearsay?

Voice your concerns about the program at the outset, add your input and then get on with it. People who bring nothing except criticism to the discussion will inevitably end up marginalized. Remember that improvements in the development process have to be made to work by YOU. So YOU have to be positive. YOU have to want to improve.

Consider also the fact that if you don't take part then you will have to deal with other peoples' ideas on how you should do your work.

If others are for it, but you don't see the need for improvement, then you should consider the very real possibility that you might well be part of the problem. In any case, if you're not convinced then you must say so. (But remain open to persuasion by your peers. After all, *you* are open—minded aren't you?)

Heroes are the ones out in front; not those back in the trench complaining their boots are too tight…

PROBLEMS

Try and use the program to solve some of your day-to-day problems but don't forget that solving *your* problem could cause a problem for somebody else.

I've found the problem-solving approach to improvement works well, particularly for Practitioners. Solving Practitioners' problems might not always fit well with the overall approach, nor is it always going to move in quite the right direction, but it can certainly be used as a starting point.

For example, a workshop with the following agenda would kick-start any program on a local basis:

- What are the objectives of the improvement program?

- What are our biggest problems?

- How do we Practitioners prioritize those?

- What do we Practitioners think could be done to solve these problems?

- How do these problems fit to the improvement program/model?

In my experience, if you take an honest approach and a cross-section of Practitioners, you will usually come up with a pretty good mix of problems. Your list will provide useful input to the program, or you can set about addressing the problems yourself and ask for support from the Improvers as necessary. Make sure they are aware of what you're doing anyway—invite them to your meeting and fit in with the overall plans.

Take the initiative!

PROCESS

Try and think in terms of process and blank out everything else. It's not always easy to make that split. Consider what it is that you do (not what the end result is) and whether there's a better way of doing it.

It will help if you make a conscious effort to consider improvement issues away from your usual work environment. When you're wrapped up in your work, it's very difficult to split out process from product, but it's something that you have to do it in order to improve your processes. Or, I should say, in order to improve your processes *successfully*. If you don't make this split when you're trying to identify areas for improvement, there's a danger that your revised processes won't work any better than the current set.

As well as splitting how you do things from the things that you produce, you also need to consider whether something is actually part of your process, or whether it is simply *supporting* the process. Tools fall into this category and any process that is tool-dependent is likely to have flaws. Tools *support* your process, as do templates, guidelines, etc. The process is the steps you take to achieve your product and it is with these that you have to be satisfied before you change any of the things supporting your process.

Break processes down to their "natural" level and do it progressively—strip away a level at a time. You can do it top-down (preferable) or bottom-up (probably easier) but don't mix up process items that belong at different levels.

Always think purely in terms of improving process.

PROFESSIONAL

Lastly, be professional. Whether you like to admit it or not, you're in business to provide your customers with what they want, not to use the latest technology or sexiest tool. If it's good for the customer then it's good for the business, and you have to find a way of incorporating it in your process or product. But not at any price. Such changes need to be made in a controlled way and that includes changes to your process.

Don't change things just for the sake of changing them and always consider the effects of process change on the product. Does it *really* make sense to introduce a new tool at this stage of the project or should we curb our natural techie desire for the latest technology and concentrate on satisfying our customer instead?

Technical people tend to be easily influenced by technological advances and can let themselves down badly as a result. Yes, that new compiler might well be free of those annoying faults that the previous version had, but do you really need to add the risk of new, unknown problems to those already existing on your current development project?

Demand from yourself what you demand from others...

Responsibility Table for PRACTITIONERS

Requirement → Role	Policymakers	Managers	Practitioners	Improvers
PQ34—What is my motivation for doing this?			10	
[Note 1] PQ35—What benefits will I see from it?"			10	
[Note 2] PQ 36—Where do I have the most problems?			10	
[Note 2] PQ37—Where do I "make do and mend" in my processes?			10	
[Note 2] PQ38—Where do I have to circumvent "the system" because the system's too damn slow or simply doesn't work?			10	
[Note 3] PQ39—Where am I "getting away with it"?			10	

Notes to the Table

Note 1—Note that there is a subtle difference between this and "what benefits will I GET". Are those benefits enough to convince you to at least go along with the program? If not, say so!

Note 2—How can these things be improved? Whoops! Watch out—now you're in the improvement business!

Note 3—Be honest. If you're cheating, does it make sense to carry on doing so or should you take the lead and try and get things changed so you don't have to cheat any more?

Improvers' Part

What I'm describing here ought to dovetail pretty well with just about any quality or improvement model you care to name, at least it does with all those I currently know about. However, the documents you need in order to start implementing most models will take up a few acres of desk space. I would recommend that you mind your Ps& Qs to lay solid foundations for your program, and then move on to actually implementing your chosen model or standard.

Some of these Ps & Qs are preparatory, others are things you need to be attending to throughout the life of your program. It should be obvious which are which and I didn't want to set up any delineations. Just as you should refer back to your improvement model for advice as you go, so you should refer back to this section of the book as your program progresses to refresh your memory and check you're not missing something.

PREPARE (YOURSELF)

As well as the things outlined in the Prepare chapter, there are some PQs which you need to answer before you get too deeply involved in your improvement activities. There is a degree of overlap with other PQs, but I have included these separately here because of their importance to you. As well as *preparing*, you have to *be prepared for* your role as an Improver. The following PQs may seem somewhat simplistic, but you must at least relate them to your own situation.

Exactly what you need to do to make sure you are prepared is obviously dependent upon you and the program you are involved in, but until you can honestly answer "YES" to these questions, then you're *not* prepared and you must take steps to *get* prepared.

PQ40—Am I comfortable with my role?

PQ41—Am I ready to rumble?

PREPARE (YOUR PROCESS)

As well as general preparation, you have to prepare your process before you can make any changes. There are three "traditional" steps to this and they work so I won't try and re-invent them:

1. Investigate what exists and analyze what doesn't work the way it should. *("Where are we?")*

2. Decide on what is required. *("Where do we want to be?")*

3. Plan how to get from what exists to what is required. *("How do we get there?")*

This means that you have to describe the existing process, find out what the requirements are for this process, and then describe the desired process and the steps that need to be taken in order to realize it.

If nothing exists, then Step 1 is fairly easily done, although you need to be wary. You could fail to recognize something that actually fills the role of a process but isn't described as such. Processes aren't always described in nice neat manuals. Often, you will find *de facto* processes in peoples' heads, defunct manuals, plans, memos, or scribbled on a beer mat propping up the corner of somebody's desk.

Take care to seek out all relevant inputs to this preparation, and avoid extra effort later.

PILOT

Once you've prepared your process, whether new or revised, then you can introduce it to your expectant colleagues. Unless the process is very localized, you should first pilot it. I don't just mean localized in application, but also in *effect*. A process might only be applied by one person, but can have a wide effect on others. You have to introduce it in a controlled and *restricted* way. Maybe to one project or area. Sometimes you might be able to do it with just one individual, obviously this will depend on the process and your organization.

As well as a restricted area of application, your pilot should have a time restriction. It's usually quite easy to pilot things on development projects as you can limit their scope to a particular phase, release, project, whatever you want as long as it makes sense.

Obviously, your piloting needs to fit with the work being done. If you want to pilot a way of gathering customer requirements, there's little point trying to do it with a project which is in its testing phase, so you need to consider when you're deciding on what processes to improve first when you would actually be able to pilot them. This might change your priorities.

PROVE

The point of piloting is to prove your process works as intended by monitoring its use and supporting the users in its application.

At the end of the pilot phase, you sit down with the process users and learn any lessons, refine the process and maybe start over. It shouldn't be your decision that the effectiveness of a process is, or is not yet, proven, rather a consensus between yourself and users.

Don't be impatient. It might take several iterations before you have a process description worthy of the name, particularly if nobody is too sure when you start exactly what it is you're talking about. Don't get downhearted either—it's not a negative reflection on your abilities if it takes time to get it right.

Proving processes doesn't stop. Depending on the process, there are going to be ways you can monitor its ongoing effectiveness. For example, you can check for yourself in project repositories how widely some processes—a document template, coding guidelines, etc., are being applied and how effectively.

PROMULGATE

Once your process has been successfully piloted and proven, then you can introduce it for general use. Before you can do this, you must do some more preparation, the extent of which will depend upon on how many people have to know about the process.

The process description will need to be done in the way that is usual in your organization. You may have a Quality Manual, a Development Handbook, or some other recognized reference document, a web site or other information repository.

My favored method of introduction is to have a full and approved process description enhanced by one or more *aides memoir*, usually a severely abridged version of the full process description. Even the most weighty of process tomes can be cut to an A4 page containing the really basic information. You can produce several of these to suit different roles or perspectives, maybe as printed cards or web pages with specific views.

For example, a planning process could have views, or cards, for each of the roles described in the process, typically line managers, project managers, planners, users. They all have to use the process but do different things with it.

I always make sure that the potential users of a process are given every opportunity to comment on it before it is "signed off". Having users involved in piloting and proving will help but their real value is in having them introduce the changes to their peers. Those users not involved will always want to know why you did or didn't do this or that, and their colleagues are the best people to explain those things.

Use existing regular meetings—team, project, department—to make a presentation on the basic facts about the process, what it means to the audience and where they can find out more. Issue your *aides memoir*—or tell people of their location (e.g. URL)—at these meetings. Don't waste time going through all the ins and outs of the process, just a short presentation giving the bare facts, and then follow up with individuals, or in the same meetings, to see how the process is doing.

Follow-up is just as important to successful promulgation as how you do the introduction. Go along to team meetings to discuss how people are finding the change. Ask for feedback, no, *seek out feedback*—if it doesn't come to you, go get it. You can't improve if you don't know what's wrong.

Your aim, when promulgating a process, must be to make the users own it. If you don't, it will always be seen as *your* process and weaker as a result.

PREPARE—PILOT—PROVE—PROMULGATE

A podful of Ps to apply to your process! You may well have seen this similarly described elsewhere but probably not quite so prettily put. Whether you are creating or revising a process, you need to carry out these steps.

They are iterative and you should take as many iterations of the first three steps as you need before moving on to the fourth.

PARADIGM

I hate this word. Hell, for me, would be having to write mission statements using the word "paradigm" as often as possible.

Be that as it may, it fits here. Before you dash off trying to fulfill the requirements of whichever model your boss just attended a seminar about, or that you want to get onto your profile, you do need to make sure that the model fits your needs.

Maybe you need more than one, or there is an industry-specific version that would apply to your work better than the generic version. Spend some time in making sure, even if you end up by simply reinforcing your original decision.

PQ42—What really is the correct improvement model for us?

(BE) PERCEPTIVE

You have to be able to see all sides of any particular discussion. You *must* listen to other peoples' views and take them into account. The expectations and perspectives of a particular process can differ greatly between—for example—Managers and Practitioners.

Remember too, that there are different sets of requirements for just about every process and you have to cover them all and—because of your role—*understand* them all. As a Practitioner, you might find the needs of the quality group for information from a process a nuisance, but those needs are just as relevant to the overall success of the process as any others.

When trying to satisfy these differing requirements, always refer back to the program's objectives and the model(s) you are working to and you won't go far wrong.

(BE) PASSIONATE

You have to believe in what you're doing. If *you* don't get excited about it, don't be surprised if others don't.

(BE) PERSUASIVE

But always be ready to compromise. There is, despite what feline fanciers will tell you, always more than one way to skin a cat...

PRAGMATIC/PRACTICAL

Improvements really do have to have to fit with THE REAL WORLD. It's your job to make sure that they do, as well as meeting the requirements of your improvement program objectives and model(s).

Be careful not to sacrifice quality for pragmatism though. It was insisting on living in this "real world" where rules can be bent which gave you the need to improve in the first place!

PIVOT

Make sure you—or your group if you're not a lone Improver—act as the pivot for improvement. *You* are the person others should seek out to discuss potential improvements, to question, to complain.

PRO-ACTIVE

If you are to act as the pivot for your program, then you will need to be pro-active in your approach. Take a lead in facilitating discussion about process issues, make yourself heard but make sure you listen too.

Don't wait for people to seek you out (although I hope they will)—get out and about. Talk to people, drink coffee, eat cookies, talk some more…[1]

I always know when I'm doing my job as an Improver properly because the boss keeps giving me dirty looks. Every time he sees me I'm chatting to someone beside the coffee machine. (An added bonus to being pro-active is that there are no calories in black coffee. There are other things in there though, so take care…)

PREVAIL

As the champion of improvement for your particular area, you have to prevail if your program is to succeed. Sometimes, you need to fight for quality.

You can't do this at any expense, hence the need to be pragmatic.

The fact is that you realize your own objectives in improvement through other people. Your success depends on *their* co-operation. It's not easy, but you have to make sure their objectives fit with your own or you won't win through.

---

1.   All in moderation of course!

QUANTIFY

Although this is very difficult—*and it doesn't get much easier with experience*—you have to find measurements by which you can judge the success of your process. The effectiveness of any process can be measured. A process whose success can't be quantified against a goal or standard is lacking in some way.

Metrics is a whole big subject in its own right, particularly in software development, but without a way of measuring effectiveness we have no basis for improvement. If you look at the processes you are trying to improve, you will probably find that their one common feature is that there is no objective way of knowing whether they work or not.

When thinking of process measurements, you may need to consider correlations rather than just simple data. Making such correlations allows you to better judge whether an improvement is successful as well as providing data which you can use to concentrate your own efforts where they are most needed.

You will get more adept at this over time, but look at available data from your processes from the outset and get a feel for how to measure process efficiency. (You probably will not be able to find a satisfactory way of quantifying your process until you have completed at least one PREPARE—PILOT—PROVE—PROMULGATE iteration.)

QUIDDITY

No, I'd never heard of this either so we've both learned something.

"Quiddity" means "the essential nature of something" and that's what you have to seek with Process Improvement. Always look for the simple core of any problem or process in order to find your basis for improvement. Once you've found it, then you can improve it.

Reduce any process to its simplest constituents first; make sure you've got it right and only then elaborate. (Refer back to the PROCESS section in the Practitioners' Part for more on this.)

◆   ◆   ◆

There were lots of Ps and Qs that I originally had listed in this chapter, but it would be unfair to expect you to remember them all. I have tried to include here those that I see as key to your success in the Improver role. Even so, they are enough, and I wish you luck in implementing them!

Responsibility Table for IMPROVERS

Requirement	Policymakers	Managers	Practitioners	Improvers
Note 1 PQ40—Am I comfortable with my role?				10
Note 2 PQ41—Am I ready to rumble?				10
PQ42—What really is the correct improvement model for us?				10

Note to the Table

Note 1—If not, why not? And what can I do about it?

Note 2—You might not have to physically fight anyone, but you will have to argue the case for improvement long, and often hard.

Never Mind The Quality—Feel The Width

The four roles that I have described so far are common to every improvement program, but there will be others who also have their part to play. Their importance to your program is for you to decide, but you must nevertheless include them in your plans. The size, scope and relationship—indeed *relevance*—of such staff to improvement efforts varies greatly from organization to organization, so I will only offer general advice. You must interpret that advice for your own situation. One thing you must *not* do is to underestimate the importance of these people to your efforts so think carefully now if you want to avoid problems later on.

Rather than being functions which might "deal with" development (e.g. Marketing, Production,) these are functions which either come under the same branch of the organizational tree or are linked by a dotted line. (Or should be!)

ADMINISTRATIVE STAFF

Admin people need to be kept aware of what is going on and can play an active role. For example, nobody knows the way the department works and what is going on better than the secretaries ("team assistants"—call them what you will).

Years ago, in my pre-development days, I was part of a quality improvement "circle" in a manufacturing company. One of the department heads, wishing to make it clear that he had no time for all this nonsense but at the same time having to fill the requirement to provide somebody, sent along his secretary. As a group, we talked about this (and the young lady concerned took some persuading that it could work) and we decided to play her department head's game.

The secretary became a valuable part of our team. Knowing just about everybody—and blissfully free of political shackles—she was able to talk openly to everyone in her department (thereby bringing some very worthwhile subjects for improvements) and to find out stuff which the rest of us never could. Sadly, after he noticed just how many improvement initiatives were kicking off in his own area, the manager substituted her for someone who would toe his "party line". It was fun while it lasted, and showed me how everyone can—and should—play their part when it comes to improvements.

So, think about how to make sure everyone is involved in your program in some way and not just the obvious people.

SUPPORT STAFF

It stands to reason in a research and/or development area that relies heavily on systems and tools for just about all its work, that those systems and tools need to be reliable. So, the people who provide the systems, tools and support need to be involved in your improvement program.

(This goes for other areas too and you should interpret it accordingly. In manufacturing, for example, the work on the line can only ever be as good as the machines used allow. Problems? Take a look at your machine requirements and design processes before you start whipping the operators.)

Tools should—*first and foremost*—meet the requirements of their users. This is not always the case, with IT/IM departments acting like they know everything and buying some tools based not on the requirements of users but on their own criteria. Unfortunately, they are often aided and abetted in this by Practitioners who just go for the latest thing without bothering to follow anything like the disciplined approach they insist upon from their own users. Like considering the true cost, or suitability of purpose.

The needs of both users (e.g. development staff) and suppliers (IT department) need to be met by such tools and these can sometimes seem to be incompatible. The fact is, that some of the improvements you put in place will need new tools, upgrades for others, more processing power, and so on. These things have an effect on your support staff and you have to make sure they are informed and involved at every stage. If your development and support people already talk regularly (i.e. not just *ad hoc*) then more power to you. Co-operation is what is needed and not—as I have sometimes witnessed—confrontation.

One thing you should *never* do is to change your process to suit the tool. Yes, you might have to tweak the process here and there to make it fit, but the tool should support the process, not the other way around. If you can't find a tool that fits your process, then you need to look carefully at your process again or ask whether you're considering the right type of tool at all.

A tool purchased to support one programming language might be inappropriate for another. You might well find you have to change some tools because they are not suitable—perhaps even harmful—to the efficiency of your process. Make such changes as soon as you can, with due regard to having proven your process first. For this you will have to involve support staff, who—if you've had them with you during your improvement discussions—will better understand your needs and not just reject them out of hand on seemingly arbitrary grounds.

If you don't currently have any effective controls over your development environment, then you won't get very far with most improvement models anyway, so this is an area you really can't ignore. Similarly, if your support staff don't already have their own SOPs (Standing Operational Procedures) then maybe their processes need to be improved too. To introduce some new development tools can take years, as can expensive infrastructure, so involve the right people from the start.

QUALITY FUNCTIONS

You may think from some of my comments thus far, that I have no time for quality departments. That they are all inflexible, bureaucratic, self-serving non-entities peopled by arrogant, ignorant, nincompoops whose purpose is to make the lives of poor, hard-done-by Practitioners a misery.

Well, yes, some of them are like that, but a lot of the problems one finds are actually down to the fact that these functions are manned by people. Humans…Although for a number of years now I have worked mostly in process improvement, I still work occasionally in quality management, sometimes a hybrid role involving both and it would be unfair—and unfounded—to dismiss quality professionals in such a manner. I am thinking, specifically, of the effects of what one might term "the software revolution", although I am sure there are other examples you might give from your own experience.

Increasingly, software is dominating our lives, and companies that previously thought of themselves as centers of mechanical excellence now have to come to terms with the fact that they actually produce systems, an ever greater part of which is software. Take motor vehicles for example. Motor cars are essentially the same now as when they were first produced in numbers, but in the last ten years they probably have advanced more than in the previous hundred. Thanks to software.

An industry which employs hundreds of thousands of people suddenly finds itself in a state of metamorphosis: The frightening thing for the rest of us is that its success, or otherwise, in changing directly affects our safety.

I digress, but only slightly. The automotive industry is probably the largest *obvious* example of this transition; others are hidden to us. One effect of all this change is that companies are having to come to terms with assuring the quality of products which they are not geared to cope with. This is in any case not easy, and some aspects of quality assurance work are always going to be behind the game. Keeping up with the pace of change is actually impossible if one accepts that in order to assure the quality of something we first have to know what it is we are assuring the quality of! You can't count your chickens till they're hatched...

Happily, there are more and more central quality functions in established companies which are facing up to this phenomenon, but I have worked in a number of places where they are not. The pace of technological change in software development is such that even the Practitioners themselves have trouble keeping up, so it's no wonder that quality people do too. If the quality engineers have mechanical or electronic backgrounds, if the quality function's structure is rigid and based on the company's needs five, ten, twenty years ago, then they may prove to be a major obstacle to process improvement.

People are naturally wary of change, indeed, this book is about how to tackle change simply because it is so problematic. There are two big dangers here:

- That the quality function will get left behind and eventually be marginalized as things change so much that they become a redundant force;

- That a quality function, which refuses to change its ways, will win out and kill off any improvement initiatives.

Neither of these outcomes benefits the organization, so involve the quality people from the outset and find a meaningful role for them.

TESTERS

A reliance on testing to prove the worthiness of systems is usually an indication that things are going wrong elsewhere. The whole ethos of Total Quality hinges on the idea of getting things right first time rather than checking them, and then sending them back for rework as often as it takes till it's right. Or nearly right...

For those organizations that perceive the test department as the last line of defense, it is very difficult to accept that life for everybody—not least the testers themselves—will get better through improving their processes.

One system development project I worked with had 10 or so developers and one hero. The hero was the test guy who found all the bugs that slipped through the development net, and he had become the single most important element in the project's lifecycle. Each new iteration of the product brought new problems and more chances for glory for the tester. Not that he—or his colleagues—viewed it that way. It was just usual for him to find some monumental bugs which brought a sharp intake of breath followed by a sigh of relief all round.

There was virtually no in-process quality at all. The product was one of those hybrids that had started life as a largely mechanical device that, as time passed, had evolved into a system the greater part of which was software. The Practitioners had started out as mechanical or electronics engineers who now had to produce software too. Everybody was doing the best job they could, and nobody had the faintest idea that not only could they improve things but that things *needed* improving. Like most of us, they believed their approach to be "normal".

Changing attitudes is never easy, but that's what you have to do. And you have to start on changing attitudes before you start implementing process improvements. If your own organization is test-reliant then you need to be thinking about how you're going to tackle that dependency. The chances are the *status quo* serves most peoples' needs except maybe the customer. The testers probably congratulate themselves for finding bugs, the Practitioners are happy to not waste their time checking stuff and management doubtless support the whole creaky construction.

You have to change this if you are going to become truly quality-oriented and attend to the difficult enough job of improving your processes. All the time the accent is on the end of the development cycle, resources and effort will not be freed up to address the real problem areas that occur earlier. It stands to reason that if there is a hole in your bucket that you have to repair it, but if you're in the bucket making business, then you ought to try and make them all without the hole.

Some development functions seem unable to grasp this and employ lots of people to find the holes and patch up the buckets, without ever trying to stop the holes getting there in the first place. (Not just development either, in manufacturing they sometimes don't even patch the holes—they just keep throwing the buckets away!)

A good place to start to look for reasons to improve such situations is what we might call "post-production"; i.e. with what happens to your product after it leaves you. Gather some data to support your arguments—call centers, service organizations, CRM (customer relationship management) systems are usually able to offer information which you will find useful to support the argument.

Something you will need to address is what will happen to the test staff who will be effectively made redundant by your new improved development processes. In truth, it will never be as immediate as that, but you must take steps to ensure that they don't just get squeezed out and end up moving elsewhere. The least obvious solution (till you think about it), is to involve them more in design. Quality is another area where their knowledge can be brought to bear to good effect.

Finding the same problems time and again often frustrates testers, and you can use that frustration as a vehicle for your pro-change arguments. In any case, involve them early in the consultation process and listen to what they have to say—they know more about your product than just about anybody else.

Test is often one of the few places that you can get some meaningful data from your development activities. Test results can always give you *something*, and test tools often produce a mountain of data. Most of that data will be useless if it's based on testing systems which have been developed without adhering to a constant process.

Simple correlations can be made between test results and the rest of your development lifecycle. For example, you can see where the most major faults are found in a particular product (or part thereof) during test and then investigate the processes which produced that product. Follow such trails and you will find not only the cause, but also arguments to support process improvement.

Handle them right and testers can become one of the strongest weapons in your improvement armory, handle them wrong and you might never get it going…

A Plethora Of Ps & A
Quintessential Q

Finally, here they are—those that didn't quite fit elsewhere or seemed to be virtual duplicates. I threw out a lot of "Ps and Qs", but I think these are worth a mention as they reinforce what has already been written and may help you to better understand something which didn't quite make sense before.

PARTNERSHIP

I hope by now you have received the message that in order to succeed, Process Improvement needs to involve all those people who use, affect, or are affected by the process being improved. That's one of the main reasons I wrote this book—no one group can do it alone. There has to be support and input from the others for virtually every activity.

Establish every improvement activity as a partnership and strengthen your chances of success.

PERMEATE

Nobody can be quite sure how things become part of the culture of an organization, but they do. There are good practices and bad practices that are helping and hindering your organization all day, every day. Follow the guidance in these pages and make sure that you spread the good practices and spread the word of your successes.

Make every effort to ensure that your program becomes part of daily working life.

PUBLICIZE

Use every tool you have, every opportunity, to make people aware of what you are doing. In pre—email days, I used to print out snappy slogans and leave them on peoples' desks and in their mail—*Quality junk mail!*

Set your creative instincts free! Change the splash screen on your configuration management tool, add help files, have a shortcut to your web page as part of the standard desktop.

You might even have some fun, but whatever you do *make it interesting.*

PREVENT PERPLEXITY

KISS. Keep It Simple, Stupid. Forget about the stupid, just keep it as simple as possible. "It"? *Everything!*

PRECLUDE PESSIMISM

This is a beauty isn't it? Well, *I* like it…

It's surprising how quickly a few setbacks can make you think you're never going to get anywhere.

Stick with it—watch out for the doomsayers and head them off at the pass. When German (American) football teams are losing badly, their fans sing "Always Look on the Bright Side of Life". This is admirable and should be a fine example to you in your darkest hours.

PROLIFERATE

Yes, probably the same as PERMEATE, but you can see how I'm making this idea of your program becoming part of every day life lodge itself in your head can't you?

PENETRATE is a good word for this too, but you can have too much of a good thing.

PROUD

Be proud of what you achieve and make sure other people feel good about their achievements too.

In development, we're above all that whooping and yelling and "Lowest Error Rate Code of the Month" type stuff, but celebrate your successes and recognize achievement.

You must also take care not to turn people off, though. There are some sensitive folks in development, excessive celebration might be OK for those financial types, but we have our brain cells to think of...

PARLEY

Often you have to compromise, but never lose sight of your objectives.

I'm sure Confucius said this before and much more succinctly, but as long as you are still headed for your destination the exact route and the speed don't matter too much.

You're in this for the long haul—so give a little, you can afford magnanimity, you have right on your side!

◆   ◆   ◆

And finally, the most important of them all. I wish you good luck in your efforts, it won't be easy, but it *will* be worthwhile. Whatever else you do, just make sure you...

Never QUIT!

APPENDIX A

Responsibility Table

This appendix contains a composite of all the responsibility tables contained in the book and is intended for use as an aid *after you have read the book*. It's an aid—I make no great claims for it. You might find it helpful, maybe not; it's up to you. Asking the questions at all is what matters.

Agree the responsibilities before you start implementation.

- Read

- Discuss

- Consult the table

- Agree responsibilities

- Implement your Program

Please use the Responsibility Table as a simple tool to provide you with a starting point for improvement. It must not be used as replacement for the real nitty-gritty of planning, answering most of the PQs being a pre-cursor to that work.

Although some PQs are quite subjective and may even appear nebulous, you have to find a way of applying them in a concrete way to your improvements. The table allows you to decide who has to answer the question and their answers are the input to your planning. In other words, answers have to be found and translated into terms relevant to your program and to the organization.

For example, take PQ05—"What is the Scope of our program?" This has been weighted (5) for Policymakers to answer, but they can't answer it alone. Their perspective and understanding of apparently well defined things such as organization structures won't take into account the shoehorning that may have had to be done at lower levels. What might have appeared a simple enough thing—"we apply it to X"—will only work if "X" actually means "X" to everyone involved. It often doesn't in practice.

Now, you may have already started work on improving, say, your requirements management, and be holding regular workshops and the like. The decision has to be made whether that work will come under your program banner or will continue as it is. In PQ07 you have to capture all those things which can be understood as process or quality improvement, and think about how to integrate them. Do you *want* to integrate them? *Should* you integrate them?

These are innocent questions which often bring unwanted answers and that's why you have to tackle them before you start. How they relate to your planning can be seen in Appendix B—Improvement Planning.

In the composite table there are additional columns so that responsibilities for Managers, Practitioners and Improvers may be split to reflect your organization's needs. (If you have to think about why I haven't split the Policymakers responsibilities then you really *do* need this book!)

I have included my suggested weightings from the individual chapter tables for guidance. Regardless of how big your organization is, I believe you should keep the splitting of responsibilities to a minimum, so you must equate these extra columns to your own organization and then split the weighting or just use the originals. For example, you might like to identify project leaders as one level of practitioner responsibility.

If you have to take a matrix management approach, then you can split between project and line management, or whatever makes sense. As long as it makes sense to everybody, otherwise you might just be adding to your problems!

It's up to you exactly how you use it—the important thing is that when using the table, you identify who does what and make sure your planning and implementation reflects this initial focus point.

Composite Responsibility Table

Requirement	Policymakers	Managers	Practitioners	Improvers
PQ01—How do we build a team (teams) for this program?	1	3	1	2
PQ02—What skills and resources do we need?	2	3	2	3
PQ03—What are the likely risks to our program?	3	4	1	2
PQ04—How do we incorporate our program into the usual processes?	4	4	3	2
PQ05—What is the Scope of our program?	3	3	1	1
PQ06—What should we call our program?	3	2	2	4
PQ07—How does our program fit to existing initiatives?	3	3	3	3
PQ08—Is there any synergy or other benefits to be had?	3	3	0	4
PQ09—How will we fit our program to the organization with maximum benefit and minimum upset?	4	2	1	3
PQ10—How do we publicize and institutionalize the program?	4	3	1	2
PQ11—Why are we doing this?	3	3	3	1
PQ12—What can we reasonably expect to achieve?	2	2	2	4
PQ13—How will we identify and measure our success?	4	3	2	2
PQ14—How can we make sure this reaches all the people we want it to reach?	3	3	3	3
PQ15—What are the current costs of not getting it right first time?	3	3	0	4
PQ16—Do we want to use these costs as the focus for our program?	4	2	1	3
PQ17—If "YES" to PQ16, how do we do that?	2	3	1	4

Requirement	Role Policymakers	Managers	Practitioners	Improvers
PQ18—*Are* all concerned 100% ready for this?				
PQ19—If "NO" to PQ18, what are their doubts/needs and how can they be addressed?				
PQ20—Do I promise to tell the truth, the whole truth and nothing but the truth?				
PQ21—How independent can our program be without becoming an orphan?				
PQ22—What mechanisms can we use to ensure that our program will always be considered and not just killed during a re-organization?				
PQ23—How will we identify and manage risks which arise during the life of the program?				
PQ24—How many levels of implementation will we have?				
PQ25—How will we resource our teams?				
Note 1 TOTALS (Excluding role-specific PQs)				

Note to the Table

Note 1 Just for fun! I never planned these numbers to come out any particular way, but they do show how important it is to involve the Improvers in setting up your program! Too often they aren't. If you have used your own weightings, and they are significantly different to mine, then you should make sure you're not simply covering up for somebody who doesn't want to be involved. 10—20% difference—no problem. If more than 20%, then look again!

Requirement	Policymakers	Managers	Practitioners	Improvers
PQ26—How can I make sure the right people are involved?	•			
PQ27—What happened to those previous programs that fell within our definition of "Process Improvement"?	•			
PQ28—What do I want to have reported to me, how and when?	•			
PQ29—Are my pants fireproof?	•			
PQ30—What do I still need to do to empower the people who have to implement the improvements and to ensure they will be supported as the program progresses?	•			
PQ31—How high a priority can we assign to this work?		•		
PQ32—Who will get the job done?		•		
PQ33—Where can I get involved and add some value?		•		
PQ34—What is my motivation for doing this?			•	
PQ35—What benefits will I see from it?"			•	
PQ36—Where do I have the most problems?			•	
PQ37—Where do I "make do and mend" in my processes?			•	
PQ38—Where do I have to circumvent "the system" because the system's too damn slow or simply doesn't work?			•	
PQ39—Where am I "getting away with it"?			•	
PQ40—Am I comfortable with my role?				•
PQ41—Am I ready to rumble?				•
PQ42—What really is the correct improvement model for us?				•

APPENDIX B

Improvement Planning

I got into Process Improvement when I set out to produce a project plan for a software development project and found that I had no basis for doing so. There was no defined project lifecycle, no defined processes, nobody quite sure what was to be expected and when. So I set about defining a development lifecycle.

Never did get the plan done...

Maybe because I come from a planning background, I tend to easily spot errors in plans. Unfortunately, modern planning tools allow you to do things in ways that are contrary to the planning logic on which they are based. Mostly, they give you warning when you try this, but people still overload resources 3 or 400% to make the red line fit their deadline, forget they did it, then wonder why they can't keep to their schedule and why the staff are all off sick.

The convention that is most often ignored is the most basic one. There is an order to planning, and that order is Tasks—Duration—Resources. If you do it in any other order, you are only making life harder for yourself.

The logic you must apply when planning is that you have unlimited time and resources. Only when you reach the point where you have entered all your tasks and durations, *and are confident that you've got them right*, do you start assigning resources and making *reasoned* adjustments to your schedule. Those adjustments need to be reason*able* too, i.e. humanly possible.

Often you may know that you're going to use a particular resource for a task because he's the only guy who can do the job, but that doesn't alter the basic logic. Your estimates of duration should be what you expect the "average" resource, working alone, would take. If you apply such a set of basic assumptions to all your projects then everyone understands what is behind the plan and can work with it.

Too often, management simply don't trust the plans they receive, and too often the facts that the plans present, i.e. "it's going to take us till Christmas next year" are simply swept aside—"you have three months". It's better not to plan at all than do that. Any time you spend on the plan after that kind of arbitrary judgment will be wasted, as was the time you spent preparing it.

I offer this as bonus advice because you should be seeking to set an example to the rest of the organization in the way you do things in your program. Make sure you apply best practice to your improvement planning. You might have to learn, but that's what Process Improvement is all about—the recognition of the need for and implementation of improvements.

Types of Planning

Different improvement models demand different things by way of planning, if anything.

If we accept that Policymakers, Managers and Practitioners operate at three levels of an improvement "hierarchy", then we can fit our planning to that.

You should be able to fit these three levels to your own organization easily enough. The SEI's CMM ® also identifies three levels of planning for improvement activities—*Strategic, Tactical* and *Activity*. My three levels are purely hierarchical and so can relate to the organization any way you want, including the CMM approach if it suits you. The levels I've defined reflect a "traditional" approach to planning, being essentially Program—Project—Task.

However you use them, the levels should provide you with those links to the "real world" which are so important if your program is to be accepted within the organization.

Those typical "real world" links are shown in the table on the next page. This is only an example—you have to make it fit to your own organization. Regardless of how you do it, your program needs to relate to the things in the third column *somehow*, and if you plan them in from the outset, it will be easier than having people make their own assumptions.

Table Relating Planning To The Organization

Planning Level	Relates to the Organization at	Refer (Link) To	Ps & Qs Role
One	Top Level (Company or Business Unit)	Business Objectives (e.g. Mission Statement).	Policymakers and Improvers
Two	Development Unit, Group, Project level.	Budget Plans, Unit/Project Resource Plans, Quality Objectives, Management Meetings.	Managers and Improvers
Task	Sub-project/Practitioner level.	Relevant Resource Plans, Technical forums.	Improvers and Practitioners (Implementation Teams)

Level One Planning

At the top level, the need is to define the framework in which the program will operate. The danger here is to be *too detailed* (and thereby take away peoples' freedom to make it work the way they want to) or *too vague* (and thereby fail to give the program the support it needs).

The following are the key components of planning at the top level:

- Objectives.

- Budget.

- Priorities.

- Scope.

You can, quite easily, make the whole program one of your Overall Business Objectives for the coming year (assuming you issue annual objectives), viz.:

"The [Insert snappy program acronym here] program is Priority A for next year. The overall objective is for all software development units to reach Level 2 on the SEI CMM® and in order to achieve this, all such units are

expected to spend 5% of their budget on implementing and supporting the program. All units are to carry out a self-assessment against the CMM in Q3."

You will recall my plea not to place arbitrary targets on people. Adding the words "by year end" after "SEI CMM" is not advised. You may, however, include such targets where they have been properly analyzed by the people expected to achieve them, or are based on an independent assessment or audit.

The assessment mentioned in the last sentence of our objective would give you the basis for demanding more exact requirements the following year.

The above statement of your objective would need to be supported by the relevant budget allocations and a code for people to book their work to, but it fills the Level One planning need. It tells people what is expected and shows support without unnecessary constraint.

Level Two Planning

This is the first level of "nitty-gritty" planning. This is where you say what will happen to the 5%! Here, you need to make sure that your improvement program (maybe sub-divided into projects at this level—which equates to development units remember) fits into your normal pattern of running projects. You have to apply the same processes to it as you would to any other project.

The most important thing is to give people what they need in order to get the job done. That means:

- Identifying priorities between this and other projects and between activities within the program.
- Budget Planning.
- Resource Planning.
- Dependencies.
- Risk Analysis.
- Planning and Reporting Requirements.
- Responsibilities.

Although you might do budget planning on an annual basis, I would recommend only planning in detail at this level for a maximum of six months. If there is a dependency on one particular implementation team getting a result first and that team will work for four months, then your plan should only run for four months before being reviewed and renewed.

The *really* important thing is to ensure that the hard-won budget for improvement activities isn't lost. That means being pragmatic in your planning. Recognize that if Project X is key to the firm's survival, then you won't be able to do much work on improvement till that's done, but then make improvement top priority.

This really is the most difficult thing in Process Improvement for Managers. If you allow the improvement program to slip down the priority list now—for any reason, good or bad—then you may be condemning it to a slow, painful, death. It's time to gird your loins, assign those resources and make damned sure they work on the improvement activities that you and the Improvers have identified as priority.

Remember that you are trying to improve quality for your customer, and that the payback for you is in freeing up resources in future because they won't be spending their time putting right what went wrong. This is "man or mouse" time. If, at the end of the year your improvement budget has been spent on other work and nobody seems to care too much because we got Project X done even if it was three months late, it's time to break out the cheese…

Task Level Planning

This has to be done. Properly. No excuses. Usually—although not exclusively—this means planning the work of implementation teams. The Improvers should also produce their own low-level planning and there is no reason why both should not use the same template.

It always pays to do these things in the most *sensible* way. I would suggest that rather than an overall plan for each team, that the team produces a plan for how they expect to realize each objective allocated to them, as they will probably tackle one thing at a time!

Each such plan has to include the following:

- Objective.
- Task list.
- Responsibilities.
- Resource Plan.

- Dependencies.

- Risks.

- Budget Plan.

- References.

- Interfaces.

Using your regular planning tool could combine some of these, but I would always list the tasks and identify resources in a document anyway and use the tool's output for tracking purposes. (Not everyone needs to know your detailed resource planning, but they will want to know who is responsible for what and what tasks are involved.)

Before you start planning, you need to produce the template for these plans and some guidelines on how to use it. Make it as simple to use as you possibly can, without sacrificing the need for a complete description of what is to be done.

Planning Documentation

As well as whatever documentation your usual program administration requires, I would recommend that you produce a Process Improvement Plan (PIP) document. It can be done on the web now, of course. However you do it, it should be printable so people can take it with them in planes, trains and automobiles. (Well, maybe not automobiles unless you put a disclaimer on the front about it being company policy to discourage reading while driving.)

Your PIP will contain a summary of what the program is about, references to the relevant higher level plan, activities for the period the plan covers and all the task level plans. Your first version will not include all the task level plans—the plan should be updated as these are approved and issued.

"Approved"?! Well, you didn't think I was going to let you get away with that did you? Before implementation managers and Improvers must approve activity plans. Managers must not take that as an excuse to kill things. ("Sorry, I don't have time right now—it will have to wait a couple of weeks".) Deadlines for producing and approving plans must be agreed in advance of planning commencing.

There can be several levels of PIP depending on how big your program is, but they always come from the top down and reference back from the bottom-up. That way, individuals can always find how their own work fits with the program. The table on the following page gives an example of how this works.

Table of Planning Levels Relationships

The Level One Plan might state	"Optimizing the way we recognize and ensure implementation of customer requirements is our top Process Improvement area for the coming year."
The Level Two Plan would include such things as	Reference to the Business Objective. Improvement Activities: • Establish a Requirements Gathering Process. • Improve Customer Acceptance Procedures. • Etc.
There would be a number of Task Plans, each referring back to the Level Two Plan item (Establish a Requirements Gathering Process) for such things as	Investigate current method and Recommend Changes. Analyze the need for a tool to help in gathering requirements and evaluate possible tools for suitability. Tool Evaluation. Etc.

Relating Planning to the PQs

With some PQs there is a relationship with planning, mostly at the top level, which will result in something being included in your plan. Although that relationship exists, the PQs are primarily intended to make you *think* and when you act you should refer back to them and think about what they mean to you.

PQ05—"What is the Scope of our program", for example has an obvious direct relationship, but as a PQ it is intended as a pre-cursor to any planning process and not as part of it.

By all means, use the PQs as a check that you have planned all those things in, but don't try and relate them all directly. It might drive you mad…

Appendix C

Implementation Teams

The work described in this appendix should mostly be done by the Improvers, although members of the Preparation Team can play a useful role in explaining the program, and management must play its part by way of allocating resources, smoothing feathers, etc.

◆   ◆   ◆

You will have gathered by now that what you do before you start your program is important. Indeed, I believe preparation to be just as key to your chances of success as actually implementing the program. It follows, therefore, that how you prepare your implementation is pretty important too!

There are 5 things to take into consideration when forming implementation teams.

1. Look at what exists and decide how to fit it into your program.

2. Decide on the team's structure and membership.

3. Formalize the team's way of working.

4. Hold a kick-off meeting.

5. Have the team do their detailed planning.

These things should be done in this order, and I would recommend producing a brief procedural document describing this framework in terms of its application to your program. It should be applied to all teams that you subsequently set up. Like other work, it helps when people don't have to re-invent wheels, but can quickly be productive in a new team because they already learned how such groups work.

Look At What Exists

As we saw in Appendix B—Improvement Planning, implementation teams come from your planning, not the other way around. Having said that, I wrote earlier in the book that you should fit your program with anything that exists.

In just about every place I've worked, I've found something already existing which could be interpreted as an improvement implementation team, even if not actually identified as such. There are often regular meetings or workshops on aspects of development process or tools, and if you look closely at them you will find that their brief (where it exists) includes Process Improvement. They might not see it that way, and it might not be a big part of what they do, but it almost certainly is there.

You may need to put a lot of effort into this phase, for example if a group exists which is working in an area identified as a priority for your program. Their *raison d'être* might be that nobody was attending to this problem, so they took it into their own hands. They might need a lot of persuading that you're not just going to steal their thunder or make them do things your way.

Some such groups even operate covertly and might take some flushing out. Sometimes, you will find they welcome you with open arms because, if you've followed the advice in this book, you will be able to offer them the chance to make their work "official" and thereby get the necessary resources allocated.

You need to do three things with such extant groups:

- Tell them what you intend to achieve with your program.

- Let *them* decide—after you've given them all the facts—how they might fit into it.

- Make sure the relationship is defined and that there is a link between the work of the group and your program *in every case*.

Take care that your program doesn't threaten anything that is, or could be, involved in Process Improvement, no matter how small its contribution.

Ideally, subject-specific groups will be absorbed into your program, but in the first place, just acknowledging their existence and defining their relationship with your program will probably be enough. Meetings where Process Improvement is simply discussed (e.g. management meetings, quality forums) must at least incorporate a feedback mechanism with the program and can be very useful for reviewing suggestions, identifying areas for improvement and so on.

I know that this might be a little confusing, because of what I wrote in the Prepare chapter, and you might have gotten the idea that fitting with existing efforts was a one-off preparatory task. In truth, like most things in quality, you need to be constantly reviewing the situation, especially since people may use the impetus of your program to start their own initiatives.

So, once you've decided on what activities are required and how best to do them, then you have to look again—even if you think you know the answer from your preparation—at what exists by way of current efforts.

Team Structure and Membership

Some improvement models advocate the use of working groups, usually along the lines of ongoing technical forums. My approach is less restricted and I really don't mind what people use such groups (here called Implementation Teams) for.

As long as they have a defined role and objectives, do the required planning and aren't just discussion groups, they can be "permanent" or just explore a specific topic for a few days worth of effort.

Exactly what roles each team needs will be dependent on its brief. There are some roles that have to be filled though:

1. Sponsor—the person or group (e.g. management meeting) from which the team gets its objectives and deadlines.

2. Leader—The team must have a named leader, or spokesperson, whose job it is to lead meetings and report back to the sponsor.

3. Expert—A person with expertise and experience in the subject[1].

4. Innocent—A person with no specific expertise or experience in the subject[2].

Roles 1 & 2, 2 & 4 may be combined. Roles 2 & 3 must *not*[3].

---

1. "Experience", if it's something new to you all, could just mean "has read the book" or "done the training".
2. The fresh view—somebody who won't make all the usual assumptions and who *will* ask the "stupid" questions.
3. Hell hath no fury like a guru scorned. If the experts were getting it right, you wouldn't need to look at it.

The sponsor could be a central Implementation Team and this team's leader a member of that central team. That approach works well, but you must make sure you bring in new blood and spread the skills around.

If you don't have somebody in mind, then let the group elect its own leader. Having said, that, the leader must be somebody with the personal attributes necessary to effectively chair meetings. (Training people to run meetings is a good area for spending some of that hard won improvement budget. Payback will come not just in your implementation teams but in everyday work too.)

How you make up the rest of the team is up to you. Include your cynics in these teams as well as "believers". Make sure there is a balance between the two. One of each in a team is enough to ensure healthy debate without facilitating time-wasting squabbling.

The optimum size of such teams is five people. Eight is the absolute maximum and I always groan inwardly when I discover myself sitting in such a large—or larger—group. You know how it is in big meetings—some people just have to try to make their mark even if they have nothing to say, while others simply say nothing.

Improvement teams are working groups, and working groups *work*. Size is a barrier to that. People have to learn to trust others to represent them in such teams.

Way of Working

Because I've found getting people together to solve problems to be a great way of implementing change, I try not to impose too many rules on such teams. There has to be a certain level of discipline, however, or you run the risk of setting a bad example, which is not a good thing for an improvement program to do.

The following is the framework I usually set for such teams. I've found it to work well because—like the best development processes—it allows people freedom to do things the way they want, while providing others with insight into what they are doing. The rules are:

- The team's sponsor must set specific objectives and "deliverables"[1].

---

1.   Also known as "work products" and by other names. Whatever you call them, they are the things—recommendation, presentations, documents, flowcharts, plans, whatever—that the group has to produce.

- The team must have deadlines for achieving their objectives and deliverables.

- The team does its own planning on how it will achieve the deadlines set for it.

- The team keeps concise records of its meetings and work.

- The team reports regularly as required by the sponsor.

Don't make deadlines unreasonable, but don't make them easy either. The group will get its act together a lot quicker when under *some* pressure.

Lessons can be learned from team reports for other teams—you should be seeking to improve your implementation team processes too! There is usually some existing forum, e.g. a management meeting, where reports can be given in the form of a presentation and discussion rather than in writing. The presentation should be able to stand—alone as a report though as you might like to widen its distribution beyond the meeting.

Kick-Off

Every new team—regardless of whether the members have previous experience in another team or not—should adhere to the same broad agenda for a kick-off meeting. As with reporting, there may be an existing medium that would serve well for the kick-off, e.g. monthly meeting.

As well as the team itself, other interested parties may attend to reinforce the importance of the occasion. A short address by "the boss" by way of introduction will help[1] as will a representative from a relevant higher level implementation team (e.g. line of business).

There should be a "standing" agenda for implementation team kick-off meetings that can then be added to as required for each new team. The standing agenda could be:

1. A short introduction (probably by an Improver) explaining about the overall program, implementation teams and how they work.

2. Briefing by the Team Leader on what this particular Implementation Team is expected to achieve with reference to any relevant information.

---

1. Just so long as (s)he then stays for the duration and doesn't rush off to the next motivational exercise!

3. Administrative details—how to book time spent, expenses, etc.

4. Question and Discussion Session. (This item gives the opportunity for the group to ask questions prior to any work being done. At the end of the briefing the team must be asked whether they understand the assignment and whether each individual is happy to undertake it)

5. Next steps.

Members can introduce themselves, but this is only really necessary when they don't already know each other—for example when members of external departments or suppliers are taking part.

One aim of the meeting is to give people the chance to air their views, allay fears and avoids them doing so during later meetings when they should be working. You will need to address any problems that arise. Don't be scared to start over if it isn't going to work the way you thought.

I like to assign people to read material (the time for which must be planned in to their schedules) as a first step after the Kick-Off and give them a chance to think about it, then get together a week or so later to discuss specific points. One thing for sure about Process Improvement—there's *always* something to read and plenty to discuss!

Detailed (Task Level) Planning

Is the first job for any implementation team. They need to translate their objectives into activities and this gives them the chance to decide exactly what it is they are dealing with.

For how that detailed planning is done, refer back to Task Level Planning in Appendix B—Improvement Planning.

For information, discussion and support material, visit
www.psandqs.info

0-595-27754-3

Printed in the United States
42844LVS00006B/528

9 780595 277544